C-2326 CAREER EXAMINATION SERIES

This is your
PASSBOOK for...

Nutritionist

Test Preparation Study Guide
Questions & Answers

NATIONAL LEARNING CORPORATION®

COPYRIGHT NOTICE

This book is SOLELY intended for, is sold ONLY to, and its use is RESTRICTED to individual, bona fide applicants or candidates who qualify by virtue of having seriously filed applications for appropriate license, certificate, professional and/or promotional advancement, higher school matriculation, scholarship, or other legitimate requirements of education and/or governmental authorities.

This book is NOT intended for use, class instruction, tutoring, training, duplication, copying, reprinting, excerption, or adaptation, etc., by:

1) Other publishers
2) Proprietors and/or Instructors of "Coaching" and/or Preparatory Courses
3) Personnel and/or Training Divisions of commercial, industrial, and governmental organizations
4) Schools, colleges, or universities and/or their departments and staffs, including teachers and other personnel
5) Testing Agencies or Bureaus
6) Study groups which seek by the purchase of a single volume to copy and/or duplicate and/or adapt this material for use by the group as a whole without having purchased individual volumes for each of the members of the group
7) Et al.

Such persons would be in violation of appropriate Federal and State statutes.

PROVISION OF LICENSING AGREEMENTS – Recognized educational, commercial, industrial, and governmental institutions and organizations, and others legitimately engaged in educational pursuits, including training, testing, and measurement activities, may address request for a licensing agreement to the copyright owners, who will determine whether, and under what conditions, including fees and charges, the materials in this book may be used them. In other words, a licensing facility exists for the legitimate use of the material in this book on other than an individual basis. However, it is asseverated and affirmed here that the material in this book CANNOT be used without the receipt of the express permission of such a licensing agreement from the Publishers. Inquiries re licensing should be addressed to the company, attention rights and permissions department.

All rights reserved, including the right of reproduction in whole or in part, in any form or by any means, electronic or mechanical, including photocopying, recording, or by any information storage and retrieval system, without permission in writing from the Publisher.

Copyright © 2025 by
National Learning Corporation

212 Michael Drive, Syosset, NY 11791
(516) 921-8888 • www.passbooks.com
E-mail: info@passbooks.com

PASSBOOK® SERIES

THE *PASSBOOK® SERIES* has been created to prepare applicants and candidates for the ultimate academic battlefield – the examination room.

At some time in our lives, each and every one of us may be required to take an examination – for validation, matriculation, admission, qualification, registration, certification, or licensure.

Based on the assumption that every applicant or candidate has met the basic formal educational standards, has taken the required number of courses, and read the necessary texts, the *PASSBOOK® SERIES* furnishes the one special preparation which may assure passing with confidence, instead of failing with insecurity. Examination questions – together with answers – are furnished as the basic vehicle for study so that the mysteries of the examination and its compounding difficulties may be eliminated or diminished by a sure method.

This book is meant to help you pass your examination provided that you qualify and are serious in your objective.

The entire field is reviewed through the huge store of content information which is succinctly presented through a provocative and challenging approach – the question-and-answer method.

A climate of success is established by furnishing the correct answers at the end of each test.

You soon learn to recognize types of questions, forms of questions, and patterns of questioning. You may even begin to anticipate expected outcomes.

You perceive that many questions are repeated or adapted so that you can gain acute insights, which may enable you to score many sure points.

You learn how to confront new questions, or types of questions, and to attack them confidently and work out the correct answers.

You note objectives and emphases, and recognize pitfalls and dangers, so that you may make positive educational adjustments.

Moreover, you are kept fully informed in relation to new concepts, methods, practices, and directions in the field.

You discover that you are actually taking the examination all the time: you are preparing for the examination by "taking" an examination, not by reading extraneous and/or supererogatory textbooks.

In short, this PASSBOOK®, used directedly, should be an important factor in helping you to pass your test.

NUTRITIONIST

DUTIES

Under general supervision of a higher-level professional nutritionist, provides nutrition services and education as part of an overall departmental program, including developing and implementing nutritional care plans, providing diet counseling to individuals and conducting group nutrition education programs, in order to improve participants' health and nutrition and to promote their healthy growth and development. Participates in in-service training programs for agency staff and may supervise paraprofessionals or students who assist in nutrition education and activities, and subordinate clerical and technical personnel. Work is performed in an automated systems environment. Does related work as required.

SCOPE OF THE EXAMINATION

The <u>written test</u> will cover knowledge, skills and/or abilities in such areas as:

1. Educating and interacting with others;
2. Basic and advanced nutrition and dietetics;
3. Patient/client dietary care; and
4. Preparing written material.

HOW TO TAKE A TEST

I. YOU MUST PASS AN EXAMINATION

A. WHAT EVERY CANDIDATE SHOULD KNOW

Examination applicants often ask us for help in preparing for the written test. What can I study in advance? What kinds of questions will be asked? How will the test be given? How will the papers be graded?

As an applicant for a civil service examination, you may be wondering about some of these things. Our purpose here is to suggest effective methods of advance study and to describe civil service examinations.

Your chances for success on this examination can be increased if you know how to prepare. Those "pre-examination jitters" can be reduced if you know what to expect. You can even experience an adventure in good citizenship if you know why civil service exams are given.

B. WHY ARE CIVIL SERVICE EXAMINATIONS GIVEN?

Civil service examinations are important to you in two ways. As a citizen, you want public jobs filled by employees who know how to do their work. As a job seeker, you want a fair chance to compete for that job on an equal footing with other candidates. The best-known means of accomplishing this two-fold goal is the competitive examination.

Exams are widely publicized throughout the nation. They may be administered for jobs in federal, state, city, municipal, town or village governments or agencies.

Any citizen may apply, with some limitations, such as the age or residence of applicants. Your experience and education may be reviewed to see whether you meet the requirements for the particular examination. When these requirements exist, they are reasonable and applied consistently to all applicants. Thus, a competitive examination may cause you some uneasiness now, but it is your privilege and safeguard.

C. HOW ARE CIVIL SERVICE EXAMS DEVELOPED?

Examinations are carefully written by trained technicians who are specialists in the field known as "psychological measurement," in consultation with recognized authorities in the field of work that the test will cover. These experts recommend the subject matter areas or skills to be tested; only those knowledges or skills important to your success on the job are included. The most reliable books and source materials available are used as references. Together, the experts and technicians judge the difficulty level of the questions.

Test technicians know how to phrase questions so that the problem is clearly stated. Their ethics do not permit "trick" or "catch" questions. Questions may have been tried out on sample groups, or subjected to statistical analysis, to determine their usefulness.

Written tests are often used in combination with performance tests, ratings of training and experience, and oral interviews. All of these measures combine to form the best-known means of finding the right person for the right job.

II. HOW TO PASS THE WRITTEN TEST

A. NATURE OF THE EXAMINATION

To prepare intelligently for civil service examinations, you should know how they differ from school examinations you have taken. In school you were assigned certain definite pages to read or subjects to cover. The examination questions were quite detailed and usually emphasized memory. Civil service exams, on the other hand, try to discover your present ability to perform the duties of a position, plus your potentiality to learn these duties. In other words, a civil service exam attempts to predict how successful you will be. Questions cover such a broad area that they cannot be as minute and detailed as school exam questions.

In the public service similar kinds of work, or positions, are grouped together in one "class." This process is known as *position-classification*. All the positions in a class are paid according to the salary range for that class. One class title covers all of these positions, and they are all tested by the same examination.

B. FOUR BASIC STEPS

1) Study the announcement

How, then, can you know what subjects to study? Our best answer is: "Learn as much as possible about the class of positions for which you've applied." The exam will test the knowledge, skills and abilities needed to do the work.

Your most valuable source of information about the position you want is the official exam announcement. This announcement lists the training and experience qualifications. Check these standards and apply only if you come reasonably close to meeting them.

The brief description of the position in the examination announcement offers some clues to the subjects which will be tested. Think about the job itself. Review the duties in your mind. Can you perform them, or are there some in which you are rusty? Fill in the blank spots in your preparation.

Many jurisdictions preview the written test in the exam announcement by including a section called "Knowledge and Abilities Required," "Scope of the Examination," or some similar heading. Here you will find out specifically what fields will be tested.

2) Review your own background

Once you learn in general what the position is all about, and what you need to know to do the work, ask yourself which subjects you already know fairly well and which need improvement. You may wonder whether to concentrate on improving your strong areas or on building some background in your fields of weakness. When the announcement has specified "some knowledge" or "considerable knowledge," or has used adjectives like "beginning principles of..." or "advanced ... methods," you can get a clue as to the number and difficulty of questions to be asked in any given field. More questions, and hence broader coverage, would be included for those subjects which are more important in the work. Now weigh your strengths and weaknesses against the job requirements and prepare accordingly.

3) Determine the level of the position

Another way to tell how intensively you should prepare is to understand the level of the job for which you are applying. Is it the entering level? In other words, is this the position in which beginners in a field of work are hired? Or is it an intermediate or advanced level? Sometimes this is indicated by such words as "Junior" or "Senior" in the class title. Other jurisdictions use Roman numerals to designate the level – Clerk I, Clerk II, for example. The word "Supervisor" sometimes appears in the title. If the level is not indicated by the title, check the description of duties. Will you be working under very close supervision, or will you have responsibility for independent decisions in this work?

4) Choose appropriate study materials

Now that you know the subjects to be examined and the relative amount of each subject to be covered, you can choose suitable study materials. For beginning level jobs, or even advanced ones, if you have a pronounced weakness in some aspect of your training, read a modern, standard textbook in that field. Be sure it is up to date and has general coverage. Such books are normally available at your library, and the librarian will be glad to help you locate one. For entry-level positions, questions of appropriate difficulty are chosen – neither highly advanced questions, nor those too simple. Such questions require careful thought but not advanced training.

If the position for which you are applying is technical or advanced, you will read more advanced, specialized material. If you are already familiar with the basic principles of your field, elementary textbooks would waste your time. Concentrate on advanced textbooks and technical periodicals. Think through the concepts and review difficult problems in your field.

These are all general sources. You can get more ideas on your own initiative, following these leads. For example, training manuals and publications of the government agency which employs workers in your field can be useful, particularly for technical and professional positions. A letter or visit to the government department involved may result in more specific study suggestions, and certainly will provide you with a more definite idea of the exact nature of the position you are seeking.

III. KINDS OF TESTS

Tests are used for purposes other than measuring knowledge and ability to perform specified duties. For some positions, it is equally important to test ability to make adjustments to new situations or to profit from training. In others, basic mental abilities not dependent on information are essential. Questions which test these things may not appear as pertinent to the duties of the position as those which test for knowledge and information. Yet they are often highly important parts of a fair examination. For very general questions, it is almost impossible to help you direct your study efforts. What we can do is to point out some of the more common of these general abilities needed in public service positions and describe some typical questions.

1) General information

Broad, general information has been found useful for predicting job success in some kinds of work. This is tested in a variety of ways, from vocabulary lists to questions about current events. Basic background in some field of work, such as sociology or economics, may be sampled in a group of questions. Often these are principles which have become familiar to most persons through exposure rather than through formal training. It is difficult to advise you how to study for these questions; being alert to the world around you is our best suggestion.

2) Verbal ability

An example of an ability needed in many positions is verbal or language ability. Verbal ability is, in brief, the ability to use and understand words. Vocabulary and grammar tests are typical measures of this ability. Reading comprehension or paragraph interpretation questions are common in many kinds of civil service tests. You are given a paragraph of written material and asked to find its central meaning.

3) Numerical ability

Number skills can be tested by the familiar arithmetic problem, by checking paired lists of numbers to see which are alike and which are different, or by interpreting charts and graphs. In the latter test, a graph may be printed in the test booklet which you are asked to use as the basis for answering questions.

4) Observation

A popular test for law-enforcement positions is the observation test. A picture is shown to you for several minutes, then taken away. Questions about the picture test your ability to observe both details and larger elements.

5) Following directions

In many positions in the public service, the employee must be able to carry out written instructions dependably and accurately. You may be given a chart with several columns, each column listing a variety of information. The questions require you to carry out directions involving the information given in the chart.

6) Skills and aptitudes

Performance tests effectively measure some manual skills and aptitudes. When the skill is one in which you are trained, such as typing or shorthand, you can practice. These tests are often very much like those given in business school or high school courses. For many of the other skills and aptitudes, however, no short-time preparation can be made. Skills and abilities natural to you or that you have developed throughout your lifetime are being tested.

Many of the general questions just described provide all the data needed to answer the questions and ask you to use your reasoning ability to find the answers. Your best preparation for these tests, as well as for tests of facts and ideas, is to be at your physical and mental best. You, no doubt, have your own methods of getting into an exam-taking mood and keeping "in shape." The next section lists some ideas on this subject.

IV. KINDS OF QUESTIONS

Only rarely is the "essay" question, which you answer in narrative form, used in civil service tests. Civil service tests are usually of the short-answer type. Full instructions for answering these questions will be given to you at the examination. But in case this is your first experience with short-answer questions and separate answer sheets, here is what you need to know:

1) Multiple-choice Questions

Most popular of the short-answer questions is the "multiple choice" or "best answer" question. It can be used, for example, to test for factual knowledge, ability to solve problems or judgment in meeting situations found at work.

A multiple-choice question is normally one of three types—
- It can begin with an incomplete statement followed by several possible endings. You are to find the one ending which *best* completes the statement, although some of the others may not be entirely wrong.
- It can also be a complete statement in the form of a question which is answered by choosing one of the statements listed.

- It can be in the form of a problem – again you select the best answer.

Here is an example of a multiple-choice question with a discussion which should give you some clues as to the method for choosing the right answer:

When an employee has a complaint about his assignment, the action which will *best* help him overcome his difficulty is to
- A. discuss his difficulty with his coworkers
- B. take the problem to the head of the organization
- C. take the problem to the person who gave him the assignment
- D. say nothing to anyone about his complaint

In answering this question, you should study each of the choices to find which is best. Consider choice "A" – Certainly an employee may discuss his complaint with fellow employees, but no change or improvement can result, and the complaint remains unresolved. Choice "B" is a poor choice since the head of the organization probably does not know what assignment you have been given, and taking your problem to him is known as "going over the head" of the supervisor. The supervisor, or person who made the assignment, is the person who can clarify it or correct any injustice. Choice "C" is, therefore, correct. To say nothing, as in choice "D," is unwise. Supervisors have and interest in knowing the problems employees are facing, and the employee is seeking a solution to his problem.

2) True/False Questions

The "true/false" or "right/wrong" form of question is sometimes used. Here a complete statement is given. Your job is to decide whether the statement is right or wrong.

SAMPLE: A roaming cell-phone call to a nearby city costs less than a non-roaming call to a distant city.

This statement is wrong, or false, since roaming calls are more expensive.

This is not a complete list of all possible question forms, although most of the others are variations of these common types. You will always get complete directions for answering questions. Be sure you understand *how* to mark your answers – ask questions until you do.

V. RECORDING YOUR ANSWERS

Computer terminals are used more and more today for many different kinds of exams.

For an examination with very few applicants, you may be told to record your answers in the test booklet itself. Separate answer sheets are much more common. If this separate answer sheet is to be scored by machine – and this is often the case – it is highly important that you mark your answers correctly in order to get credit.

An electronic scoring machine is often used in civil service offices because of the speed with which papers can be scored. Machine-scored answer sheets must be marked with a pencil, which will be given to you. This pencil has a high graphite content which responds to the electronic scoring machine. As a matter of fact, stray dots may register as answers, so do not let your pencil rest on the answer sheet while you are pondering the correct answer. Also, if your pencil lead breaks or is otherwise defective, ask for another.

Since the answer sheet will be dropped in a slot in the scoring machine, be careful not to bend the corners or get the paper crumpled.

The answer sheet normally has five vertical columns of numbers, with 30 numbers to a column. These numbers correspond to the question numbers in your test booklet. After each number, going across the page are four or five pairs of dotted lines. These short dotted lines have small letters or numbers above them. The first two pairs may also have a "T" or "F" above the letters. This indicates that the first two pairs only are to be used if the questions are of the true-false type. If the questions are multiple choice, disregard the "T" and "F" and pay attention only to the small letters or numbers.

Answer your questions in the manner of the sample that follows:

32. The largest city in the United States is
    A. Washington, D.C.
    B. New York City
    C. Chicago
    D. Detroit
    E. San Francisco

1) Choose the answer you think is best. (New York City is the largest, so "B" is correct.)
2) Find the row of dotted lines numbered the same as the question you are answering. (Find row number 32)
3) Find the pair of dotted lines corresponding to the answer. (Find the pair of lines under the mark "B.")
4) Make a solid black mark between the dotted lines.

VI. BEFORE THE TEST

Common sense will help you find procedures to follow to get ready for an examination. Too many of us, however, overlook these sensible measures. Indeed, nervousness and fatigue have been found to be the most serious reasons why applicants fail to do their best on civil service tests. Here is a list of reminders:

- Begin your preparation early – Don't wait until the last minute to go scurrying around for books and materials or to find out what the position is all about.
- Prepare continuously – An hour a night for a week is better than an all-night cram session. This has been definitely established. What is more, a night a week for a month will return better dividends than crowding your study into a shorter period of time.
- Locate the place of the exam – You have been sent a notice telling you when and where to report for the examination. If the location is in a different town or otherwise unfamiliar to you, it would be well to inquire the best route and learn something about the building.
- Relax the night before the test – Allow your mind to rest. Do not study at all that night. Plan some mild recreation or diversion; then go to bed early and get a good night's sleep.
- Get up early enough to make a leisurely trip to the place for the test – This way unforeseen events, traffic snarls, unfamiliar buildings, etc. will not upset you.
- Dress comfortably – A written test is not a fashion show. You will be known by number and not by name, so wear something comfortable.

- Leave excess paraphernalia at home – Shopping bags and odd bundles will get in your way. You need bring only the items mentioned in the official notice you received; usually everything you need is provided. Do not bring reference books to the exam. They will only confuse those last minutes and be taken away from you when in the test room.
- Arrive somewhat ahead of time – If because of transportation schedules you must get there very early, bring a newspaper or magazine to take your mind off yourself while waiting.
- Locate the examination room – When you have found the proper room, you will be directed to the seat or part of the room where you will sit. Sometimes you are given a sheet of instructions to read while you are waiting. Do not fill out any forms until you are told to do so; just read them and be prepared.
- Relax and prepare to listen to the instructions
- If you have any physical problem that may keep you from doing your best, be sure to tell the test administrator. If you are sick or in poor health, you really cannot do your best on the exam. You can come back and take the test some other time.

VII. AT THE TEST

The day of the test is here and you have the test booklet in your hand. The temptation to get going is very strong. Caution! There is more to success than knowing the right answers. You must know how to identify your papers and understand variations in the type of short-answer question used in this particular examination. Follow these suggestions for maximum results from your efforts:

1) Cooperate with the monitor

The test administrator has a duty to create a situation in which you can be as much at ease as possible. He will give instructions, tell you when to begin, check to see that you are marking your answer sheet correctly, and so on. He is not there to guard you, although he will see that your competitors do not take unfair advantage. He wants to help you do your best.

2) Listen to all instructions

Don't jump the gun! Wait until you understand all directions. In most civil service tests you get more time than you need to answer the questions. So don't be in a hurry. Read each word of instructions until you clearly understand the meaning. Study the examples, listen to all announcements and follow directions. Ask questions if you do not understand what to do.

3) Identify your papers

Civil service exams are usually identified by number only. You will be assigned a number; you must not put your name on your test papers. Be sure to copy your number correctly. Since more than one exam may be given, copy your exact examination title.

4) Plan your time

Unless you are told that a test is a "speed" or "rate of work" test, speed itself is usually not important. Time enough to answer all the questions will be provided, but this does not mean that you have all day. An overall time limit has been set. Divide the total time (in minutes) by the number of questions to determine the approximate time you have for each question.

5) **Do not linger over difficult questions**

If you come across a difficult question, mark it with a paper clip (useful to have along) and come back to it when you have been through the booklet. One caution if you do this – be sure to skip a number on your answer sheet as well. Check often to be sure that you have not lost your place and that you are marking in the row numbered the same as the question you are answering.

6) **Read the questions**

Be sure you know what the question asks! Many capable people are unsuccessful because they failed to *read* the questions correctly.

7) **Answer all questions**

Unless you have been instructed that a penalty will be deducted for incorrect answers, it is better to guess than to omit a question.

8) **Speed tests**

It is often better NOT to guess on speed tests. It has been found that on timed tests people are tempted to spend the last few seconds before time is called in marking answers at random – without even reading them – in the hope of picking up a few extra points. To discourage this practice, the instructions may warn you that your score will be "corrected" for guessing. That is, a penalty will be applied. The incorrect answers will be deducted from the correct ones, or some other penalty formula will be used.

9) **Review your answers**

If you finish before time is called, go back to the questions you guessed or omitted to give them further thought. Review other answers if you have time.

10) **Return your test materials**

If you are ready to leave before others have finished or time is called, take ALL your materials to the monitor and leave quietly. Never take any test material with you. The monitor can discover whose papers are not complete, and taking a test booklet may be grounds for disqualification.

VIII. EXAMINATION TECHNIQUES

1) Read the general instructions carefully. These are usually printed on the first page of the exam booklet. As a rule, these instructions refer to the timing of the examination; the fact that you should not start work until the signal and must stop work at a signal, etc. If there are any *special* instructions, such as a choice of questions to be answered, make sure that you note this instruction carefully.

2) When you are ready to start work on the examination, that is as soon as the signal has been given, read the instructions to each question booklet, underline any key words or phrases, such as *least, best, outline, describe* and the like. In this way you will tend to answer as requested rather than discover on reviewing your paper that you *listed without describing*, that you selected the *worst* choice rather than the *best* choice, etc.

3) If the examination is of the objective or multiple-choice type – that is, each question will also give a series of possible answers: A, B, C or D, and you are called upon to select the best answer and write the letter next to that answer on your answer paper – it is advisable to start answering each question in turn. There may be anywhere from 50 to 100 such questions in the three or four hours allotted and you can see how much time would be taken if you read through all the questions before beginning to answer any. Furthermore, if you come across a question or group of questions which you know would be difficult to answer, it would undoubtedly affect your handling of all the other questions.

4) If the examination is of the essay type and contains but a few questions, it is a moot point as to whether you should read all the questions before starting to answer any one. Of course, if you are given a choice – say five out of seven and the like – then it is essential to read all the questions so you can eliminate the two that are most difficult. If, however, you are asked to answer all the questions, there may be danger in trying to answer the easiest one first because you may find that you will spend too much time on it. The best technique is to answer the first question, then proceed to the second, etc.

5) Time your answers. Before the exam begins, write down the time it started, then add the time allowed for the examination and write down the time it must be completed, then divide the time available somewhat as follows:
    - If 3-1/2 hours are allowed, that would be 210 minutes. If you have 80 objective-type questions, that would be an average of 2-1/2 minutes per question. Allow yourself no more than 2 minutes per question, or a total of 160 minutes, which will permit about 50 minutes to review.
    - If for the time allotment of 210 minutes there are 7 essay questions to answer, that would average about 30 minutes a question. Give yourself only 25 minutes per question so that you have about 35 minutes to review.

6) The most important instruction is to *read each question* and make sure you know what is wanted. The second most important instruction is to *time yourself properly* so that you answer every question. The third most important instruction is to *answer every question*. Guess if you have to but include something for each question. Remember that you will receive no credit for a blank and will probably receive some credit if you write something in answer to an essay question. If you guess a letter – say "B" for a multiple-choice question – you may have guessed right. If you leave a blank as an answer to a multiple-choice question, the examiners may respect your feelings but it will not add a point to your score. Some exams may penalize you for wrong answers, so in such cases *only*, you may not want to guess unless you have some basis for your answer.

7) Suggestions
    a. Objective-type questions
        1. Examine the question booklet for proper sequence of pages and questions
        2. Read all instructions carefully
        3. Skip any question which seems too difficult; return to it after all other questions have been answered
        4. Apportion your time properly; do not spend too much time on any single question or group of questions

5. Note and underline key words – *all, most, fewest, least, best, worst, same, opposite,* etc.
6. Pay particular attention to negatives
7. Note unusual option, e.g., unduly long, short, complex, different or similar in content to the body of the question
8. Observe the use of "hedging" words – *probably, may, most likely,* etc.
9. Make sure that your answer is put next to the same number as the question
10. Do not second-guess unless you have good reason to believe the second answer is definitely more correct
11. Cross out original answer if you decide another answer is more accurate; do not erase until you are ready to hand your paper in
12. Answer all questions; guess unless instructed otherwise
13. Leave time for review

b. Essay questions
1. Read each question carefully
2. Determine exactly what is wanted. Underline key words or phrases.
3. Decide on outline or paragraph answer
4. Include many different points and elements unless asked to develop any one or two points or elements
5. Show impartiality by giving pros and cons unless directed to select one side only
6. Make and write down any assumptions you find necessary to answer the questions
7. Watch your English, grammar, punctuation and choice of words
8. Time your answers; don't crowd material

8) Answering the essay question

Most essay questions can be answered by framing the specific response around several key words or ideas. Here are a few such key words or ideas:

M's: manpower, materials, methods, money, management
P's: purpose, program, policy, plan, procedure, practice, problems, pitfalls, personnel, public relations

  a. Six basic steps in handling problems:
   1. Preliminary plan and background development
   2. Collect information, data and facts
   3. Analyze and interpret information, data and facts
   4. Analyze and develop solutions as well as make recommendations
   5. Prepare report and sell recommendations
   6. Install recommendations and follow up effectiveness

  b. Pitfalls to avoid
   1. *Taking things for granted* – A statement of the situation does not necessarily imply that each of the elements is necessarily true; for example, a complaint may be invalid and biased so that all that can be taken for granted is that a complaint has been registered

2. *Considering only one side of a situation* – Wherever possible, indicate several alternatives and then point out the reasons you selected the best one
3. *Failing to indicate follow up* – Whenever your answer indicates action on your part, make certain that you will take proper follow-up action to see how successful your recommendations, procedures or actions turn out to be
4. *Taking too long in answering any single question* – Remember to time your answers properly

IX. AFTER THE TEST

Scoring procedures differ in detail among civil service jurisdictions although the general principles are the same. Whether the papers are hand-scored or graded by machine we have described, they are nearly always graded by number. That is, the person who marks the paper knows only the number – never the name – of the applicant. Not until all the papers have been graded will they be matched with names. If other tests, such as training and experience or oral interview ratings have been given, scores will be combined. Different parts of the examination usually have different weights. For example, the written test might count 60 percent of the final grade, and a rating of training and experience 40 percent. In many jurisdictions, veterans will have a certain number of points added to their grades.

After the final grade has been determined, the names are placed in grade order and an eligible list is established. There are various methods for resolving ties between those who get the same final grade – probably the most common is to place first the name of the person whose application was received first. Job offers are made from the eligible list in the order the names appear on it. You will be notified of your grade and your rank as soon as all these computations have been made. This will be done as rapidly as possible.

People who are found to meet the requirements in the announcement are called "eligibles." Their names are put on a list of eligible candidates. An eligible's chances of getting a job depend on how high he stands on this list and how fast agencies are filling jobs from the list.

When a job is to be filled from a list of eligibles, the agency asks for the names of people on the list of eligibles for that job. When the civil service commission receives this request, it sends to the agency the names of the three people highest on this list. Or, if the job to be filled has specialized requirements, the office sends the agency the names of the top three persons who meet these requirements from the general list.

The appointing officer makes a choice from among the three people whose names were sent to him. If the selected person accepts the appointment, the names of the others are put back on the list to be considered for future openings.

That is the rule in hiring from all kinds of eligible lists, whether they are for typist, carpenter, chemist, or something else. For every vacancy, the appointing officer has his choice of any one of the top three eligibles on the list. This explains why the person whose name is on top of the list sometimes does not get an appointment when some of the persons lower on the list do. If the appointing officer chooses the second or third eligible, the No. 1 eligible does not get a job at once, but stays on the list until he is appointed or the list is terminated.

X. HOW TO PASS THE INTERVIEW TEST

The examination for which you applied requires an oral interview test. You have already taken the written test and you are now being called for the interview test – the final part of the formal examination.

You may think that it is not possible to prepare for an interview test and that there are no procedures to follow during an interview. Our purpose is to point out some things you can do in advance that will help you and some good rules to follow and pitfalls to avoid while you are being interviewed.

What is an interview supposed to test?

The written examination is designed to test the technical knowledge and competence of the candidate; the oral is designed to evaluate intangible qualities, not readily measured otherwise, and to establish a list showing the relative fitness of each candidate – as measured against his competitors – for the position sought. Scoring is not on the basis of "right" and "wrong," but on a sliding scale of values ranging from "not passable" to "outstanding." As a matter of fact, it is possible to achieve a relatively low score without a single "incorrect" answer because of evident weakness in the qualities being measured.

Occasionally, an examination may consist entirely of an oral test – either an individual or a group oral. In such cases, information is sought concerning the technical knowledges and abilities of the candidate, since there has been no written examination for this purpose. More commonly, however, an oral test is used to supplement a written examination.

Who conducts interviews?

The composition of oral boards varies among different jurisdictions. In nearly all, a representative of the personnel department serves as chairman. One of the members of the board may be a representative of the department in which the candidate would work. In some cases, "outside experts" are used, and, frequently, a businessman or some other representative of the general public is asked to serve. Labor and management or other special groups may be represented. The aim is to secure the services of experts in the appropriate field.

However the board is composed, it is a good idea (and not at all improper or unethical) to ascertain in advance of the interview who the members are and what groups they represent. When you are introduced to them, you will have some idea of their backgrounds and interests, and at least you will not stutter and stammer over their names.

What should be done before the interview?

While knowledge about the board members is useful and takes some of the surprise element out of the interview, there is other preparation which is more substantive. It *is* possible to prepare for an oral interview – in several ways:

1) Keep a copy of your application and review it carefully before the interview

This may be the only document before the oral board, and the starting point of the interview. Know what education and experience you have listed there, and the sequence and dates of all of it. Sometimes the board will ask you to review the highlights of your experience for them; you should not have to hem and haw doing it.

2) Study the class specification and the examination announcement

Usually, the oral board has one or both of these to guide them. The qualities, characteristics or knowledges required by the position sought are stated in these documents. They offer valuable clues as to the nature of the oral interview. For example, if the job involves supervisory responsibilities, the announcement will usually indicate that knowledge of modern supervisory methods and the qualifications of the candidate as a supervisor will be tested. If so, you can expect such questions, frequently in the form of a hypothetical situation which you are expected to solve. NEVER go into an oral without knowledge of the duties and responsibilities of the job you seek.

3) Think through each qualification required

Try to visualize the kind of questions you would ask if you were a board member. How well could you answer them? Try especially to appraise your own knowledge and background in each area, *measured against the job sought*, and identify any areas in which you are weak. Be critical and realistic – do not flatter yourself.

4) Do some general reading in areas in which you feel you may be weak

For example, if the job involves supervision and your past experience has NOT, some general reading in supervisory methods and practices, particularly in the field of human relations, might be useful. Do NOT study agency procedures or detailed manuals. The oral board will be testing your understanding and capacity, not your memory.

5) Get a good night's sleep and watch your general health and mental attitude

You will want a clear head at the interview. Take care of a cold or any other minor ailment, and of course, no hangovers.

What should be done on the day of the interview?

Now comes the day of the interview itself. Give yourself plenty of time to get there. Plan to arrive somewhat ahead of the scheduled time, particularly if your appointment is in the fore part of the day. If a previous candidate fails to appear, the board might be ready for you a bit early. By early afternoon an oral board is almost invariably behind schedule if there are many candidates, and you may have to wait. Take along a book or magazine to read, or your application to review, but leave any extraneous material in the waiting room when you go in for your interview. In any event, relax and compose yourself.

The matter of dress is important. The board is forming impressions about you – from your experience, your manners, your attitude, and your appearance. Give your personal appearance careful attention. Dress your best, but not your flashiest. Choose conservative, appropriate clothing, and be sure it is immaculate. This is a business interview, and your appearance should indicate that you regard it as such. Besides, being well groomed and properly dressed will help boost your confidence.

Sooner or later, someone will call your name and escort you into the interview room. *This is it.* From here on you are on your own. It is too late for any more preparation. But remember, you asked for this opportunity to prove your fitness, and you are here because your request was granted.

What happens when you go in?

The usual sequence of events will be as follows: The clerk (who is often the board stenographer) will introduce you to the chairman of the oral board, who will introduce you to the other members of the board. Acknowledge the introductions before you sit down. Do not be surprised if you find a microphone facing you or a stenotypist sitting by. Oral interviews are usually recorded in the event of an appeal or other review.

Usually the chairman of the board will open the interview by reviewing the highlights of your education and work experience from your application – primarily for the benefit of the other members of the board, as well as to get the material into the record. Do not interrupt or comment unless there is an error or significant misinterpretation; if that is the case, do not hesitate. But do not quibble about insignificant matters. Also, he will usually ask you some question about your education, experience or your present job – partly to get you to start talking and to establish the interviewing "rapport." He may start the actual questioning, or turn it over to one of the other members. Frequently, each member undertakes the questioning on a particular area, one in which he is perhaps most competent, so you can expect each member to participate in the examination. Because time is limited, you may also expect some rather abrupt switches in the direction the questioning takes, so do not be upset by it. Normally, a board member will not pursue a single line of questioning unless he discovers a particular strength or weakness.

After each member has participated, the chairman will usually ask whether any member has any further questions, then will ask you if you have anything you wish to add. Unless you are expecting this question, it may floor you. Worse, it may start you off on an extended, extemporaneous speech. The board is not usually seeking more information. The question is principally to offer you a last opportunity to present further qualifications or to indicate that you have nothing to add. So, if you feel that a significant qualification or characteristic has been overlooked, it is proper to point it out in a sentence or so. Do not compliment the board on the thoroughness of their examination – they have been sketchy, and you know it. If you wish, merely say, "No thank you, I have nothing further to add." This is a point where you can "talk yourself out" of a good impression or fail to present an important bit of information. Remember, *you close the interview yourself*.

The chairman will then say, "That is all, Mr. _____, thank you." Do not be startled; the interview is over, and quicker than you think. Thank him, gather your belongings and take your leave. Save your sigh of relief for the other side of the door.

How to put your best foot forward

Throughout this entire process, you may feel that the board individually and collectively is trying to pierce your defenses, seek out your hidden weaknesses and embarrass and confuse you. Actually, this is not true. They are obliged to make an appraisal of your qualifications for the job you are seeking, and they want to see you in your best light. Remember, they must interview all candidates and a non-cooperative candidate may become a failure in spite of their best efforts to bring out his qualifications. Here are 15 suggestions that will help you:

1) Be natural – Keep your attitude confident, not cocky

If you are not confident that you can do the job, do not expect the board to be. Do not apologize for your weaknesses, try to bring out your strong points. The board is interested in a positive, not negative, presentation. Cockiness will antagonize any board member and make him wonder if you are covering up a weakness by a false show of strength.

2) Get comfortable, but don't lounge or sprawl

Sit erectly but not stiffly. A careless posture may lead the board to conclude that you are careless in other things, or at least that you are not impressed by the importance of the occasion. Either conclusion is natural, even if incorrect. Do not fuss with your clothing, a pencil or an ashtray. Your hands may occasionally be useful to emphasize a point; do not let them become a point of distraction.

3) Do not wisecrack or make small talk

This is a serious situation, and your attitude should show that you consider it as such. Further, the time of the board is limited – they do not want to waste it, and neither should you.

4) Do not exaggerate your experience or abilities

In the first place, from information in the application or other interviews and sources, the board may know more about you than you think. Secondly, you probably will not get away with it. An experienced board is rather adept at spotting such a situation, so do not take the chance.

5) If you know a board member, do not make a point of it, yet do not hide it

Certainly you are not fooling him, and probably not the other members of the board. Do not try to take advantage of your acquaintanceship – it will probably do you little good.

6) Do not dominate the interview

Let the board do that. They will give you the clues – do not assume that you have to do all the talking. Realize that the board has a number of questions to ask you, and do not try to take up all the interview time by showing off your extensive knowledge of the answer to the first one.

7) Be attentive

You only have 20 minutes or so, and you should keep your attention at its sharpest throughout. When a member is addressing a problem or question to you, give him your undivided attention. Address your reply principally to him, but do not exclude the other board members.

8) Do not interrupt

A board member may be stating a problem for you to analyze. He will ask you a question when the time comes. Let him state the problem, and wait for the question.

9) Make sure you understand the question

Do not try to answer until you are sure what the question is. If it is not clear, restate it in your own words or ask the board member to clarify it for you. However, do not haggle about minor elements.

10) Reply promptly but not hastily

A common entry on oral board rating sheets is "candidate responded readily," or "candidate hesitated in replies." Respond as promptly and quickly as you can, but do not jump to a hasty, ill-considered answer.

11) Do not be peremptory in your answers

A brief answer is proper – but do not fire your answer back. That is a losing game from your point of view. The board member can probably ask questions much faster than you can answer them.

12) Do not try to create the answer you think the board member wants

He is interested in what kind of mind you have and how it works – not in playing games. Furthermore, he can usually spot this practice and will actually grade you down on it.

13) Do not switch sides in your reply merely to agree with a board member

Frequently, a member will take a contrary position merely to draw you out and to see if you are willing and able to defend your point of view. Do not start a debate, yet do not surrender a good position. If a position is worth taking, it is worth defending.

14) Do not be afraid to admit an error in judgment if you are shown to be wrong

The board knows that you are forced to reply without any opportunity for careful consideration. Your answer may be demonstrably wrong. If so, admit it and get on with the interview.

15) Do not dwell at length on your present job

The opening question may relate to your present assignment. Answer the question but do not go into an extended discussion. You are being examined for a *new* job, not your present one. As a matter of fact, try to phrase ALL your answers in terms of the job for which you are being examined.

Basis of Rating

Probably you will forget most of these "do's" and "don'ts" when you walk into the oral interview room. Even remembering them all will not ensure you a passing grade. Perhaps you did not have the qualifications in the first place. But remembering them will help you to put your best foot forward, without treading on the toes of the board members.

Rumor and popular opinion to the contrary notwithstanding, an oral board wants you to make the best appearance possible. They know you are under pressure – but they also want to see how you respond to it as a guide to what your reaction would be under the pressures of the job you seek. They will be influenced by the degree of poise you display, the personal traits you show and the manner in which you respond.

ABOUT THIS BOOK

This book contains tests divided into Examination Sections. Go through each test, answering every question in the margin. We have also attached a sample answer sheet at the back of the book that can be removed and used. At the end of each test look at the answer key and check your answers. On the ones you got wrong, look at the right answer choice and learn. Do not fill in the answers first. Do not memorize the questions and answers, but understand the answer and principles involved. On your test, the questions will likely be different from the samples. Questions are changed and new ones added. If you understand these past questions you should have success with any changes that arise. Tests may consist of several types of questions. We have additional books on each subject should more study be advisable or necessary for you. Finally, the more you study, the better prepared you will be. This book is intended to be the last thing you study before you walk into the examination room. Prior study of relevant texts is also recommended. NLC publishes some of these in our Fundamental Series. Knowledge and good sense are important factors in passing your exam. Good luck also helps. So now study this Passbook, absorb the material contained within and take that knowledge into the examination. Then do your best to pass that exam.

EXAMINATION SECTION

EXAMINATION SECTION
TEST 1

DIRECTIONS: Answer the following questions directly, briefly, and succinctly.

1. Are all foods of the same importance in nutrition?
2. What is a nutrient?
3. Are all the nutrients the body needs present in foods?
4. What are the essential nutrients?
5. Is water classed as a nutrient?
6. What is meant by an adequate diet?
7. Is appetite a safe guide in choosing a diet?
8. What are food groups?
9. Why is protein particularly important in nutrition?
10. What are the building materials?

KEY (CORRECT ANSWERS)

1. No. Many foods supply several nutrients; others but a few. Some foods we value mainly for the flavor, color, and texture they provide.

2. A nutrient is a chemical substance that has its own specific function in the body and works with other nutrients for growth and for regulation of all body processes throughout the life cycle.

3. Yes, abundantly. Foods vary in the kinds and amounts of nutrient they contain, however.

4. Essential nutrients for which needed amounts have been recommended include: Protein, calcium and iron; vitamin A; three vitamins of the B-complex group (thiamine, riboflavin, niacin); and ascorbic acid (vitamin C). Fat (and fatty acids), carbohydrate, phosphorus, sodium, potassium, and other nutrients also are known to be important in the body, although no specific amounts of them have been recommended.

5. Water once was classed as a non-nutrient, but it is recognized as a nutrient in current texts. A person usually needs the equivalent of 4 to 8 glasses of water daily as water or in beverages.

6. It is one that supplies all the known essential nutrients in sufficient amounts for the maintenance of health in the normal individual.

7. Not necessarily. A haphazard diet may lack certain nutrients and supply too much of others. A satisfactory diet can be obtained from well-selected foods in the different food groups.

8. Nutritionists have made convenient groupings of foods according to their similarity of predominant nutrients. One such grouping lists: Milk group; meat group (meat, fish, poultry, eggs); vegetable-fruit group; bread-cereal group.

9. Protein is an indispensable component of every cell in the body and, after water, comprises the greatest proportion of body tissues. Protein is needed to build, maintain, and repair body tissues and to fulfill regulatory functions. It may also provide energy needed. Building materials for body protein must be supplied constantly to the body.

10. Proteins are made up of simpler units called amino acids.

TEST 2

DIRECTIONS: Answer the following questions directly, briefly, and succinctly.

1. What is meant by nonessential and essential amino acids?
2. How is protein in food evaluated?
3. Why is fat necessary to well-being?
4. What are hydrogenated fats?
5. What are unsaturated and saturated fats?
6. Are fatty acids essential in nutrition?
7. From what foods can linoleic acid be obtained?
8. How much fat should one eat daily?
9. Does carbohydrate mean sugar or starch?
10. Are carbohydrates of plant or animal origin?

KEY (CORRECT ANSWERS)

1. Some amino acids the body can make from fragments made available in the breakdown of food following digestion. They are called nonessential (or dispensable) in the sense that it is not essential that they be supplied by the foods in the diet. Eight amino acids cannot be made by the body and have to be supplied readymade from the diet. They are called essential or indispensable.

2. Protein in foods varies in quantity and in quality. Protein is considered of excellent quality, or high biological value, if it has the indispensable, or essential, amino acids in proportions needed by the body. The kinds and amounts of amino acids provided by protein of one food often complement the kinds and amounts of amino acids in protein of another food. When foods that supplement each other are eaten together, as cereal with milk, the protein mixture has a better value to the body than if each food were eaten alone.

3. Fat, a component of all body tissues, is necessary in the diet. It is a source of energy, a carrier of fat-soluble vitamins, and a source of essential fatty acids. As fat is more slowly digested than protein or carbohydrate, it has satiety value and may help deter overeating. Fat layers help conserve body heat and cushion internal organs.

4. Hydrogenation is a process by which hydrogen is added to oils to obtain a solid fat product. Margarine and shortenings are examples of hydrogenated fates.

5. A fat is described by the chemist as unsaturated if it can combine with more hydrogen and as saturated if it cannot. Generally, unsaturated fats are liquid at room temperature, as the oils extracted from cottonseed, soybean, corn, safflower seed. Most saturated fats are solid at room temperature, as beef suet, hydrogenated vegetable fats, mutton tallow.

6. Yes. Fats provide those fatty acids regarded as necessary in nutrition and many others whose roles in nutrition are not yet known.

7. Richest sources of linoleic acid, an essential unsaturated fatty acid, are of plant origin.

8. Little is known about man's requirement for fat except that some is needed daily. No specific amounts have been recommended.

9. It includes both. Sugar, starch, and fiber (cellulose) are the principal carbohydrates.

10. Most carbohydrates are formed in plants from carbon dioxide of the air and from water, with the aid of sunlight and the green pigment, chlorophyll. Only a few foods of animal origin contain carbohydrates. Milk is one of these. More than one-third of the solid matter of milk is lactose, commonly called milk sugar.

TEST 3

DIRECTIONS: Answer the following questions directly, briefly, and succinctly.

1. Why is sugar sometimes called "quick energy"?
2. What happens to sugar and starch eaten in excess of daily needs?
3. In what foods do carbohydrates occur?
4. Does sugar have more calories than starch?
5. How much carbohydrate should be in the average daily diet?
6. Is food energy the same as calories?
7. Do the sometimes-called energy nutrients (protein, fat, carbohydrate) yield the same amount of energy?
8. What are high-calorie and low-calorie foods?
9. What are vitamins? How do they work?
10. How many vitamins are there? How are they classified?

KEY (CORRECT ANSWERS)

1. Ordinary sugar, sucrose, is quickly broken down into compounds that are readily absorbed and circulated to the various parts of the body by the blood.

2. A limited amount is held for ready use as carbohydrate. The remainder is converted to fat and stored.

3. Starch is found richly in cereal grains (rice, wheat, sorghum, corn, millet, rye). Potatoes and some other tubers and roots as well as seed of legumes have a relatively high content of starch. Sugars of several kinds are present in foods. Various sugars are naturally present in honey, fruit, vegetables, and milk. Sugar from sugarcane and sugarbeets may be highly refined for table use.

4. Weight for weight, the calories values of sugar and starch are about the same.

5. No daily amounts of carbohydrate have been recommended. Healthful diets may contain widely varying amounts of carbyhydrate. In some countries where the food supply is mainly from plant foods, the proportion of carbyhydrate in the average diet is much higher than in the United States and consists largely of starch.

6. No. The calorie is a standard unit of measure of energy produced in the metabolism of protein, fat, and carbohydrate in the body.

7. No. Weight for weight, fat yields about two and one-fourth times as many calories as protein or carbohydrates.

8. There is no exact line of demarcation. The calorie value of a food depends on its composition. In general, foods highest in calorie value are those rich in fat and low in moisture. Other concentrated sources are foods composed mainly of carbohydrate or protein or a mixture of either or both with fat. Sugars, cereals, dried fruits, and cheese are among the relatively concentrated sources of energy. Foods low in calorie value in general are those that contain large amounts of water and relatively little fat. These include many fruits and vegetables, particularly succulent vegetables.

9. Vitamins are chemical compounds that occur in foods in minute amounts and must be supplied to the body for normal functioning and development. Vitamins take part in chemical reactions that release energy from foods for use by the body, promote normal growth of different kinds of tissue, and are essential to the proper functioning of nerves and muscle. Research is constantly adding to knowledge of the many capacities in which various vitamins function.

10. At least 13 vitamins are known at present to be needed in nutrition. They are sometimes classified in two groups as fat-soluble vitamins and water-soluble vitamins. The fat-soluble group includes vitamins, A, D, E, and K. The water-soluble vitamins include ascorbic acid, thiamine, riboflavin, niacin, vitamin B_6, pantothenic acid, biotin, folic acid, and vitamin B_{12}. Choline and inositol are sometimes listed in the water-soluble group.

TEST 4

DIRECTIONS: Answer the following questions briefly, directly, and succinctly.

1. How are vitamins measured?
2. How many mineral elements are known to be needed as nutrients by the human body?
3. What are trace elements?
4. Are all the minerals the body needs present in foods?
5. In what foods does sodium occur?
6. Are the same daily amounts of essential nutrients recommended for everyone?
7. Are recommended daily dietary allowances the same as minimum daily requirements?
8. Is guidance available in planning an adequate diet from an ordinary variety of common foods?
9. Can "once a good source, always a good source" be said of nutrients in foods?
10. What kinds of losses does food undergo?

2 (#4)

KEY (CORRECT ANSWERS)

1. Today most vitamins are measured in units of weight, usually in milligrams or micrograms. One milligram is 1/1000 of a gram and one microgram is 1/1000 of a milligram, or one millionth of a gram. These are minute quantities, as 28.35 grams equal one ounce.

2. More than a dozen different minerals are known to have definite functions in the body. Those needed in appreciable amounts are calcium, phosphorus, iron, sodium chlorine, potassium, magnesium, and sulfur.

3. They are minerals needed in very small amounts. They include iodine, manganese, copper, zinc, cobalt, fluorine, molybdenum, and perhaps others.

4. Yes.

5. Sodium content of food varies widely. Ordinary table salt, baking soda, and monosodium glutamate are highly concentrated sources. Foods of animal origin (meat, fish, poultry, cheese) have more sodium than plant foods. Cured foods and other foods with salt added are generally high in sodium. Vegetables, with a few exceptions, are low in sodium. Fresh, frozen, and canned fruit is low in sodium unless it has been added in some form.

6. No. Needed amounts vary according to age, size, stage of growth, and condition of the individual. In general, the amounts are higher for rapidly growing boys and girls and pregnant and lactating women; they are lower for young children as well as for older persons.

7. No. Recommended daily dietary allowances are amounts of nutrients that are judged to be adequate for the maintenance of good nutrition in the population of the United States. The amounts are changed from time to time as newer knowledge of nutritional needs becomes available. Minimum daily requirements are amounts of various nutrients that have been established as standards for labeling food and pharmaceutical preparations for special dietary uses.

8. Yes. A leaflet on a daily food guide, bulletins on foods needed for good nutrition of young children, school children, the young couple, and older people are available.

9. No. Losses occur in the many stages from site of origin to the consumer's plate.

10. The basic losses are of two kinds: the physical loss, when edible parts, such as outer leaves of plants, outer layers of grains, the fat of meat, and various cooking liquids, are discarded; and the chemical loss that occurs naturally when food is held at elevated temperatures, when food is cut, exposing a greater surface, and when the tissues are bruised or dried.

TEST 5

DIRECTIONS: Answer the following questions directly, briefly, and succinctly.

1. Why is ascorbic acid so often cited in reporting the retention of nutrients in fruit and vegetables?
2. Is ascorbic acid the same as vitamin C?
3. Are minerals in foods more stable than vitamins?
4. How is ascorbic acid in roots and tubers affected by storage?
5. Are green spots on potatoes dangerous?
6. Does canning destroy the nutritive value of fruit and vegetables?
7. Are home-canned foods as nutritious as commercially canned foods?
8. In canned vegetables and fruit, are the nutrients in the food or in the liquid?
9. Is it safe to leave canned foods in the can?
10. Do canned fruits and vegetables lose food value on the pantry shelf?

KEY (CORRECT ANSWERS)

1. Ascorbic acid is lost more easily from most food than other important nutrients are. Means that protect ascorbic acid usually protect other water-soluble vitamins (thiamine, riboflavin, niacin) and other heat-sensitive vitamins (especially thiamine) as well.

2. Ascorbic acid is the chemical name for vitamin C.

3. Yes. The minerals are not destroyed, but the portions that pass into solution will be lost if cooking water, meat drippings, and canning liquid are discarded.

4. Prolonged storage increases the losses. For example, potatoes lose about one-half their ascorbic acid during the first 3 months in storage and about two-thirds during the first 6 months. Sweet potatoes lose about 30 to 50 percent of their ascorbic acid during the first 3 months in storage and another 10 percent by the end of 6 months.

5. Exposure to light causes green areas to develop. It is advisable to remove the green parts, although we know of no instances in which ill effects from eating these parts have been reported. Sprouts have more of the green-containing substance (solanin) than the potato, and should not be eaten.

6. Good commercial canning methods cause relatively little loss.

7. It depends. Foods of high quality canned at home under favorable conditions retain their nutrients well, but home operators and methods vary so much that it is not possible to make definite comparisons.

8. Soluble nutrients are about evenly distributed throughout the contents of the can. Drained solids make up about two-thirds of the contents; therefore, about two-thirds of the soluble nutrients would be in the food and one-third in the liquid.

9. Yes. The can is an excellent container, but food in cans should have the same care as fresh-cooked foods and be kept in a refrigerator.

10. Very little, if the storage place is cool. In a year, foods stored at a temperature under 65°F. show a small loss of ascorbic acid and thiamine, ranging from 10 to 15 percent. However, when stored at temperatures up to 80, the loss doubles, increasing to 25 percent. The loss continues as the storage period lengthens.

TEST 6

DIRECTIONS: Answer the following questions directly, briefly, and succinctly.

1. Does freezing affect the nutritive values of fruits and vegetables?
2. How are the food values of meat, poultry, and fish affected by freezing?
3. Is freezer burn harmful?
4. How should meat, fish, and poultry be thawed?
5. Is it safe to refreeze frozen foods?
6. How does cooking affect nutrients?
7. Is waterless cooking a superior method?
8. Is pressure cooking a desirable method?
9. Does cooking lock the nutrients in foods?
10. What kind of cooking utensils best conserve the nutrients in foods?

KEY (CORRECT ANSWERS)

1. Foods of high quality, frozen by good methods, retain their nutrients well. Blanching before freezing causes some loss of vitamins and minerals.

2. These foods have about the same nutritive value, frozen or fresh.

3. Freezer burn (a change of color due to loss of moisture or dehydration does not make the food unsafe to eat but results in some loss of quality. To prevent freezer burn, wrap the food in moisture-vapor-resistant wrapping material and seal the package tightly.

4. They should be thawed in the refrigerator, whenever possible. When time does not permit, they may be placed in a watertight wrapper and thawed in cold water. Direct exposure to water to hasten thawing results in some loss of flavor and nutritive value.

5. Frozen fruit, vegetables, and red meat that have been thawed and appear in good condition can safely be used or refrozen if they have been thawed and held at recommended refrigerator temperatures for not more than a few days. Repeated thawing and refreezing may impair flavor, texture, and nutritive value, particularly of fruit and vegetables.

6. Some cooking procedures result in much greater losses than others. The "three R's" of cooking to retain nutrients are: Reduce the amount of water used; reduce the length of the cooking period; and reduce the amount of food surface exposed.

7. Not necessarily. Although the amount of cooking water is small, the longer cooking period required by this method may offset the advantage of the smaller amount of water used.

8. This intensive method may overcook tender vegetables and result in loss of nutrients. If timing is carefully regulated, however, retention of nutrients may be as good by pressure cooking as by other methods.

9. No. Losses continue to the end. Cooking for one meal at a time and serving quickly is the best assurance of maximum nutritive values.

10. Any cooking utensil with a well-fitting lid is satisfactory, whether made of aluminum, enamel, glass, stainless steel, or other materials ordinarily used.

TEST 7

DIRECTIONS: Answer the following questions directly, briefly, and succinctly.

1. Do aluminum cooking utensils cause cancer?
2. Is it safe to eat raw meat?
3. Is it harmful to eat pork during the summer?
4. What are meat tenderizers and are they safe to use?
5. Is there a danger to health in raw eggs?
6. Does cooking effect the nutrient in eggs?
7. Are white-shell eggs higher in nutritive value than brown-shell eggs?
8. Is whole-wheat flour more nutritious than plain white flour?
9. What is enriched flour?
10. Are there other foods with added nutrients?

KEY (CORRECT ANSWERS)

1. No. The American Medical Association stated that this rumor has been investigated thoroughly and that there is no scientific evidence that the use of aluminum ware causes cancer or is in any way injurious to health.

2. No. Pork cooked to the well-done stage (185) carries no danger of trichinosis—a disease caused by trichinae (small worms) embedding themselves in the intestinal tract and muscles. Beef should be cooked at least to the rare done stage (internal temperature 140) to avoid infestation by a form of tapeworm called cysticercus, which is sometimes present in raw beef. Rabbit should be thoroughly cooked. Wild rabbits are often infected by Bacterium tularense, caused by certain tick bites that produce the disease, tularemia (rabbit fever), in man. Any bacteria remaining in the rabbit after skinning can be destroyed by cooking. Domestic rabbits are less likely to be affected, as their hutches are usually free from ticks.

3. No. With present-day refrigeration, pork, like other meats, may be enjoyed the year around.

4. Meat tenderizers have a basic ingredient papain, a vegetable enzyme of the tropical papaya melon. The tenderizer product may be prepared either with or without the addition of salt, spices, dextrose, and seasonings. The ingredients are harmless to the consumer when used as directed.

5. Raw eggs are not sterile and may carry Salmonella, one of the harmful bacteria. Eggs should be cooked. If the shells are cracked or badly soiled, the eggs must be thoroughly cooked.

6. Only slightly.

7. No. Color of shell is a characteristic of the breed of hen.

8. Yes. Whole-wheat flour is milled to include all parts of the wheat kernel, including the germ and outer layers, in which some nutrients are highly concentrated. White flour is milled from the endosperm, which is mainly starch. Enrichment of white flour is common now.

9. Enriched flour is refined flour to which certain vitamins and minerals are added within limits stipulated by law. Enrichment has led to great improvement in the American diet.

10. Yes, many. The first important addition of an essential nutrient to a staple article of food was addition of iodine to table salt in 1924. Vitamin A may be added to margarine in amounts set by Federal law and vitamin D to milk according to Federal or State laws. Many other foods have nutrients added in amounts that are not regulated by law. Many breakfast cereals, particularly those in ready-to-serve form, have added nutrients. Ingredients added to foods for which there are no regulations as to amounts must be named on the label.

TEST 8

DIRECTIONS: Answer the following questions directly, briefly, and succinctly.

1. Are commercial breads as nutritious as the old-fashioned loaf?
2. What is meant by a special diet?
3. Can an individual safely plan a special diet for himself?
4. Is it natural for an adult to put on weight as he grows older?
5. Is sodium necessary or harmful?
6. Are salt substitutes safe?
7. Are materials available in planning a sodium-restricted diet?
8. Is cholesterol necessary in the body?
9. What is the significance of cholesterol in the diet?
10. What are the food sources of cholesterol?

KEY (CORRECT ANSWERS)

1. Yes, in fact, today's commercial recipes have improved the nutritive value of white bread over that of the twenties.

2. Special diet is a broad term for diets planned to meet particular needs of individuals or groups. Most special diets can be based on an ordinary well-balanced diet for the nor-mal person.

3. No. A self-prescribed diet may have imbalances among nutrients or shortages of essential nutrients and lead to more serious problems than it is intended to alleviate. Special dietary planning varies widely and should be prescribed by a physician who is familiar with the needs and problems of the individual.

4. It may be natural, but it is not desirable. For best health it is recommended that a person maintain the weight that was right for his height and body build at 25 years of age. This requires gradual reduction of calories intake to meet reduced energy requirements due largely to lessening of vigorous physical activities and decreasing metabolic rate.

5. Sodium is a required nutrient in the body. The usual intake of sodium in this country is esti-mated as 3 to 7 grams a day. A person in normal health who follows good dietary practices need not be concerned about too much or too little sodium. A sodium-restricted diet should be supervised by a physician.

6. Yes, in general. However, salt substitutes vary in their chemical composition, and the kind and amount used should be determined by the physician who has evaluated both the indi-vidual's condition and the chemical composition of the salt substitute.

7. Yes. Besides the doctor's orders, material for dietary planning on different levels of sodium intake and general information on diet and heart disease are available.

8. Yes. Cholesterol, a fatlike substance present in all animal (body) tissues, is synthesized within the body in normal metabolic processes and is also supplied by foods.

9. This has not been clearly established. Low-cholesterol diets have received much attention in the treatment of atherosclerosis and cardiovascular diseases. Until more is known about possible relationships, however, foods should not be omitted from the diet because they contain cholesterol.

10. Cholesterol occurs only in products of animal origin. Concentrated sources are nerve tis-sues, as brains from calf, beef, lamb, hog; also egg yolk. Butter is a relatively concentrated source. Meat, poultry, fish and shellfish, and cheese have a fairly high content.

EXAMINATION SECTION
TEST 1

DIRECTIONS: Each question consists of a statement. You are to indicate whether the statement is TRUE (T) or FALSE (F). *PRINT THE LETTER OF THE CORRECT ANSWER IN THE SPACE AT THE RIGHT.*

1. Obesity is a form of malnutrition.   1.____
2. A pound of butter contains the equivalent number of calories as a pound of fat on your body.   2.____
3. Obesity is often inherited.   3.____
4. "Crash diets" are safe.   4.____
5. Pizza is not a nutritious snack food.   5.____
6. Sugar refined from sugar cane and sugar from sugar beets is the same.   6.____
7. Women require more iron than men.   7.____
8. Exercise is not necessary for small children.   8.____
9. The increasing practice of eating out has had a marked effect on eating habits and obesity.   9.____
10. Teas and tonics alleviate helath problems such as arthritis, diabetes, asthma and epilepsy.   10.____
11. You should always indulge a pregnant woman's weird cravings.   11.____
12. Sugar is more fattening than vegetable oil.   12.____
13. Vinegar will help you lose weight.   13.____
14. A fat baby is a healthy baby.   14.____
15. As you get older, weight tends to stay on you.   15.____
16. You have to be grossly overweight to be considered obese.   16.____
17. One can never take too many vitamins and/or minerals.   17.____
18. Taking off a pound or two of excess weight is too slow and discouraging a loss to be successful.   18.____
19. Everyone could use a dietary supplement.   19.____
20. Your diet would be better if it contained whole wheat and other dark breads rather than white bread.   20.____

KEY (CORRECT ANSWERS)

1. True. Malnutrition means "bad nutrition," and obesity is one of the major forms of malnutrition in America. It is caused by the consumption of too many calories that are inefficiently utilized by the body, and which, all too often, have little or no nutritional value.

2. True. There is no practical difference between the calories in butter, margarine, cooking fat or in the fat of your body. A pound of butter contains 3500 calories - the equivalent of the calories in a pound of fat in your body.

3. False. You do not inherit fat. What you do inherit is bone structure and, more importantly, your eating habits and attitudes toward food.

4. False. Most quick-weight loss diets omit some important nutrients. You need the four basic foods to maintain good health: dairy, meat, vegetables and fruits, and breads and cereals.

5. False. Pizza made with meat, cheese and tomatoes contains worthwhile nutrients, so you're getting some protein, calcium and iron, as well as the A, C and B complex vitamins.

6. True. Chemically, cane and beet sugars are the same.

7. True. Women should have a little more iron - not too much - during menstruation years.

8. False. Exercise is good for us at any age. (You can even exercise an infant by moving its arms and legs.) Exercise should be fun, too. It's a good practice to make your regular exercise regimen a family affair.

9. True. More starchy foods and sweets are thus consumed - not to mention the additional calories from cocktails that all too often accompany a meal consumed in a restaurant.

10. False. About ten years ago the sale of "diabetes tea" and "heart tonic" was stopped by law. All of these diseases require treatment by doctors.

11. False. Research shows that many mothers-to-be have strange cravings – called pica – for such harmful substances as dirt, starch and soap. Studies have also shown that some of the women were anemic and, once treated for the anemia, lost these cravings.

12. False. No one food is really fattening. It's how much you eat and what you eat that counts. When more calories are consumed than are expended, you put on weight. An equal weight of fat has twice the calories of any carbohydrate (such as sugar). Calorie consumption should be balanced with sufficient exercise.

13. False. While vinegar is a low-calorie food, it contains no magic potions, except for its sharp acid taste which will often deaden appetite.

14. False. There is strong evidence indicating the body develops fat cells in infancy and in later life these calls cannot be dieted away. A parent who overfeeds an infant is physically and psychologically laying the groundwork for obesity, and that child will have a very difficult time becoming and staying a thin adult.

15. True. However, the reason for this weight retention is the fact that you are still consuming the same number of calories as when you were younger and more active. As we get older and more sedentary, we require fewer calories because we don't burn up as many.

16. False. When weight reaches 20 percent or more above your "desirable" weight, there's only one word for it—and that's obese.

17. False. Vitamins are either water soluble or fat soluble. The water soluble are *B* and *C,* and any of these vitamins which are not needed are excreted from the body. Fat soluble vitamins, *A* and *D,* are stored in the body and could be toxic if taken in excess.

18. False. The loss is slow, perhaps, but not in comparison to how many years it took to gain that weight! Most doctors and nutritionists generally recommend such a rate of loss. Sensible well-regulated eating develops proper eating habits, and in turn, a successful weight-loss program. Crash diets are the most difficult to maintain.

19. False. For most of us, nutritional needs are met by eating a balanced diet of foods from the four basic food groups. If, for medical reasons, however, you are unable to eat certain foods, or you have special nutritional needs that are not met by eating such foods, then a dietary supplement might be advised. An example would be iron for women, expecially pregnant women.

20. False. Although whole wheat bread has more roughage and fiber content, enriched white bread has nearly the same nutritional value.

TEST 2

DIRECTIONS: Each question or incomplete statement is followed by several suggested answers or completions. Select the one that BEST answers the question or completes the statement. *PRINT THE LETTER OF THE CORRECT ANSWER IN THE SPACE AT THE RIGHT*

1. Which grain originated in the Americas? 1.____

    A. Millet B. Rice C. Oats D. Corn

2. Buckwheat is technically not a cereal grain. 2.____

    A. True B. False

3. *Spelt,* which is now sold in health food stores, was once the major cereal grain in Central Europe. 3.____
   It is a distant relative of

    A. rice B. oats C. wheat D. sorghum

4. If you are gluten intolerant, you should avoid foods containing 4.____

    A. wheat B. rye
    C. oats D. barley
    E. all of the above

5. Some people who are gluten intolerant can eat millet or buckwheat. But none of them can tolerate triticale. 5.____

    A. True B. False

6. If you are gluten intolerant, you can eat 6.____

    A. corn B. rice
    C. amaranth D. spelt
    E. all of the above

7. Kamut is a wheat substitute that some people who are gluten intolerant can eat. 7.____

    A. True B. False

8. Teosinte, which grows in southern Mexico, is a distant relative of 8.____

    A. rice B. buckwheat
    C. rye D. corn

9. The leading source of starch in the United States is 9.____

    A. triticale B. millet C. corn D. rice

10. The cereal grains are a rich source of complex carbohydrates. 10.____

    A. True B. False

11. Most grains are low in fat. 11.____

    A. True B. False

12. Grains are generally a poor source of 12.____

    A. pantothenic acid   B. protein
    C. calcium   D. vitamin B$_6$

13. Which grain is a poor source of lysine? 13.____

    A. Oats   B. Rye   C. Barley   D. Corn

14. Oats and oat bran are useful in lowering cholesterol levels. 14.____

    A. True   B. False

15. Although milling reduces many essential vitamins and minerals, which of these are good 15.____
    sources?

    A. Wheat bran   B. Rice polish
    C. Wheat germ   D. All of the above

16. Which mineral is often added to grain products? 16.____

    A. Magnesium   B. Iodine   C. Iron   D. Potassium

17. Sprouted grains are a good source of 17.____

    A. vanadium   B. vitamin K
    C. vitamin C   D. molybdenum

18. Because of milling, which vitamins are often added to grain products? 18.____

    A. B$_1$ B. B$_2$
    C. B$_3$ D. All of the above

19. The word *cereal* is derived from Ceres, who was the Roman goddess of agriculture. 19.____

    A. True   B. False

20. Archaeological diggings near Baghdad, Iraq, show that farmers in the region were culti- 20.____
    vating barley and wheat around

    A. 1922   B. 7000 B.C.   C. 1816   D. 1485

KEY (CORRECT ANSWERS)

1. D
2. A
3. C
4. E
5. A

6. D
7. A
8. D
9. C
10. A

11. A
12. C
13. D
14. A
15. D

16. C
17. C
18. D
19. A
20. B

EXAMINATION SECTION
TEST 1

DIRECTIONS: Each question or incomplete statement is followed by several suggested answers or completions. Select the one that BEST answers the question or completes the statement. *PRINT THE LETTER OF THE CORRECT ANSWER IN THE SPACE AT THE RIGHT.*

1. The human thyroid requires

    A. potassium
    B. carbohydrate
    C. iodine
    D. sulphur

2. The passage of dissolved food from the cavity of the alimentary canal into the bloodstream is known as

    A. assimilation
    B. anabolism
    C. catabolism
    D. osmosis

3. The enzyme which functions ONLY in an acid medium is

    A. amylopsin   B. pepsin   C. ptyalin   D. trypsin

4. The change of nutrients into protoplasm is called

    A. anabolism
    B. catabolism
    C. karyokinesis
    D. osmosis

5. Fat is digested MAINLY in the

    A. gall bladder
    B. large intestine
    C. mouth
    D. small intestine

6. The passage of digested substances into the villi for distribution through the body is called

    A. absorption
    B. metabolism
    C. anabolism
    D. peristalsis

7. Bile salts are valuable as digestive agents for fats because they

    A. supply the proper chemical medium
    B. emulsify
    C. neutralize
    D. increase surface tension

8. Flavinoids which are effective in human health are

    A. biotics
    B. bioflavinoids
    C. neoflavinoids
    D. vitamins

9. Salts which affect the alkalinity or acidity of protoplasm have

    A. osmotic action
    B. buffer action
    C. reduction
    D. condensation

10. The mineral which maintains osmotic pressure is

    A. potassium   B. sodium   C. magnesium   D. iron

11. The process of hydrogenation converts

    A. salt water to fresh water
    B. unsaturated fats to saturated fats
    C. fatty acids to cholesterol
    D. cholesterol to fatty acids

12. Amino acids are absorbed MAINLY in the

    A. intestine   B. stomach   C. pancreas   D. liver

13. Uric acid results from

    A. vitamin deficiency
    B. metabolism of purines
    C. digestion of carbohydrates
    D. injection of nicotine

14. An enzyme that produces digestion products which do not set to form a gel is

    A. protease   B. bromelin   C. diastase   D. lycine

15. As a result of the metabolic processes, the body

    A. can form protein from fat
    B. cannot form carbohydrate from protein
    C. cannot form fat from protein
    D. can form carbohydrate from protein

16. Which of the following minerals is found in GREATEST abundance in the human body?

    A. Phosphorus   B. Calcium
    C. Iron   D. Iodine

17. The enzyme of the gastric juice which aids in the digestion of milk is

    A. trypsin   B. amylopsin   C. rennin   D. ptyalin

18. The digestive enzyme which functions in an acid medium is

    A. pepsin   B. ptyalin   C. trypsin   D. amylopsin

19. Ascorbic acid is less susceptible to oxidation processes when it is

    A. alone   B. combined with an alkali
    C. combined with an acid   D. thoroughly aerated

20. In weight control, the MOST important reason of the following, for slow increase or decrease of weight is to make sure that the person

    A. is not forced to accept radical changes
    B. changes his eating pattern
    C. is allowed to adjust gradually
    D. avoids digestive upsets

21. During digestion, proteins are reduced to   21._____

    A. ascorbic acid   B. amino acids
    C. glucose   D. glycogen

22. When water is the chemical that causes changes in nutrients during digestion, the procedure is referred to as   22._____

    A. hydrocarbons   B. carbonizing
    C. hydrolysis   D. hydroponics

23. Of the following, the nutrient that does NOT act as a regulator of body processes is   23._____

    A. a vitamin   B. fat   C. water   D. a mineral

24. The glands involved in the digestion of starches are the   24._____

    A. spleen   B. salivary   C. thyroid   D. adrenal

25. Retarded digestion of cooked protein is caused by   25._____

    A. chemical change in the food
    B. physical change in the food
    C. destruction of bacteria
    D. slow cooking in moist heat

26. An important function of protein is to regulate   26._____

    A. body temperature
    B. glandular secretions
    C. specific dynamic action of foodstuffs
    D. the buffer action in the bloodstream

27. The normal source of insulin in the human body is the   27._____

    A. liver   B. thymus
    C. pancreas   D. pineal gland

28. The pathway of excretion of the nitrogenous end products of protein metabolism is the   28._____

    A. lungs   B. skin
    C. kidneys   D. large intestine

29. Carbohydrate stored in the liver is   29._____

    A. galleass   B. glycogen
    C. liepstarch   D. galactose

30. Carbohydrates are especially good for   30._____

    A. energy and endurance   B. building bones
    C. weight gain   D. Vitamin C

KEY (CORRECT ANSWERS)

1.	C	16.	B
2.	D	17.	C
3.	B	18.	A
4.	B	19.	C
5.	D	20.	B
6.	A	21.	B
7.	B	22.	C
8.	B	23.	B
9.	B	24.	B
10.	B	25.	A
11.	B	26.	D
12.	A	27.	C
13.	B	28.	C
14.	C	29.	B
15.	D	30.	A

TEST 2

DIRECTIONS: Each question or incomplete statement is followed by several suggested answers or completions. Select the one that BEST answers the question or completes the statement. *PRINT THE LETTER OF THE CORRECT ANSWER IN THE SPACE AT THE RIGHT.*

1. The digestive secretion that is acid in reaction is 1.____

   A. saliva
   B. gastric juice
   C. pancreatic juice
   D. bile

2. Enzymes 2.____

   A. cause food changes
   B. are activated by boiling
   C. dissolve osmotic membranes
   D. increase reaction at freezing point

3. An intermediate product in the digestion of starch is 3.____

   A. dextrin   B. cerine   C. maltine   D. fibrinogen

4. Amino acids are substances containing 4.____

   A. hydrogen   B. nitrogen   C. oxygen   D. carbon

5. Digestive secretions of the human body contain chemical compounds called 5.____

   A. peptones
   B. polysaccharides
   C. proteoses
   D. enzymes

6. Amino acids are absorbed through the 6.____

   A. stomach
   B. liver
   C. intestines
   D. pancreas

7. The clotting of blood is aided by 7.____

   A. phosphorus
   B. calcium
   C. iron
   D. copper

8. The mineral that is responsible for the alkaline reaction of the human blood is 8.____

   A. calcium
   B. phosphorus
   C. iodine
   D. iron

9. Digestion of food is helped by having your mealtimes 9.____

   A. hurried   B. happy   C. worried   D. exciting

10. The alternate contractions and relaxations which constitute the normal beating of the heart are dependent in part upon the presence of _____ salts. 10.____

    A. calcium
    B. calcium and sodium
    C. potassium and sodium
    D. calcium, sodium, and potassium

11. A catalytic agent that brings about the normal metabolism of carbohydrates in all cells of the body is   11.____

    A. insulin   B. riboflavin
    C. glucose   D. thiamin

12. Vitamin A helps to   12.____

    A. give energy
    B. stimulate an appetite
    C. prevent eye and nose infection
    D. aid digestion

13. The body uses calcium for making   13.____

    A. scar tissue   B. fat
    C. bone   D. fingernails

14. A partially complete protein is one which   14.____

    A. is capable of maintaining growth but not life
    B. contains all the essential amino acids except glycinine
    C. is capable of maintaining neither life nor growth
    D. is capable of maintaining life but not growth

15. Salts affecting acidity or alkalinity of protoplasm have the effect of   15.____

    A. osmotic action   B. condensation
    C. reduction   D. buffer action

16. An acid ash is yielded by body oxidation of   16.____

    A. meats   B. citrus fruits
    C. potatoes   D. cream

17. The presence of acetone in urine indicates faulty metabolism of   17.____

    A. proteins   B. carbohydrates
    C. fats   D. minerals

18. A vitamin preparation given merely to satisfy a patient is being used as a   18.____

    A. dilative   B. pacific
    C. placebo   D. tranquilizer

19. The organ, the secretion of which neutralizes some poisons and dissolves cholesterol is the   19.____

    A. spleen   B. thyroid   C. pancreas   D. liver

20. The PRINCIPAL element which maintains osmotic pressure in the human system is   20.____

    A. iron   B. potassium   C. magnesium   D. sodium

21. The nutritive value of a protein is ultimately dependent upon its

   A. digestibility
   B. meat source
   C. connective tissue content
   D. amino acid content

22. In fever conditions, the basal metabolism of a person as compared to the norm is

   A. lower   B. higher   C. constant   D. unchanged

23. Digested food is absorbed MAINLY in the

   A. small intestine   B. stomach
   C. large intestine   D. esophagus

24. The digestion of protein is accomplished by the action of the enzymes

   A. pepsin, trypsin, erepsin
   B. glycerol, lipase, amylopsis
   C. lecithin, cystine, lysine
   D. glycogen, ptyalin, galactose

25. In comparison with proteins, fats contain LESS

   A. carbon   B. hydrogen
   C. phosphorus   D. nitrogen

26. The gland which produces insulin is the

   A. spleen   B. pituitary   C. thymus   D. pancreas

27. The process of hydrogenation converts

   A. salt water to fresh water
   B. unsaturated fats to saturated fats
   C. fatty acids to cholesterol
   D. cholesterol to fatty acids

28. In the digestion of starch, an intermediate product is

   A. dextrin   B. fibrinogen
   C. cerine   D. maltine

29. Amino acids are absorbed MAINLY in the

   A. stomach   B. liver   C. pancreas   D. intestine

30. In anabolism, the number of calories yielded by one gram of hydrocarbon is

   A. six   B. seven   C. eight   D. nine

KEY (CORRECT ANSWERS)

1.	B	16.	A
2.	A	17.	C
3.	A	18.	C
4.	B	19.	D
5.	D	20.	D
6.	C	21.	D
7.	B	22.	B
8.	B	23.	A
9.	B	24.	A
10.	B	25.	D
11.	A	26.	D
12.	C	27.	B
13.	C	28.	A
14.	B	29.	D
15.	D	30.	D

EXAMINATION SECTION
TEST 1

DIRECTIONS: Each question or incomplete statement is followed by several suggested answers or completions. Select the one that BEST answers the question or completes the statement. *PRINT THE LETTER OF THE CORRECT ANSWER IN THE SPACE AT THE RIGHT.*

1. In substituting non-fat dried milk for whole milk in a reducing diet, it is important to consider that the dried milk has a lowered content of calories and also a lowered content of

    A. vitamin A
    B. calcium
    C. thiamin
    D. ascorbic acid

2. The PRIMARY role of legumes in our menus is that of providing

    A. economy and variety
    B. protein and vitamins
    C. flavor and color
    D. carbohydrate and protein

3. One pound of body fat is equivalent to APPROXIMATELY _____ calories.

    A. 1000　　B. 2000　　C. 4000　　D. 3000

4. The vitamins present in meat are, in general, limited to

    A. B-complex
    B. vitamin A
    C. ascorbic acid
    D. ergosterol

5. The nutrients MOST commonly lacking in American diets are

    A. ascorbic acid and riboflavin
    B. calcium and vitamin C
    C. protein and carbohydrates
    D. vitamin A and thiamine

6. Glucose and fructose are examples of

    A. disaccharides
    B. polysaccharides
    C. saccharines
    D. monosaccharides

7. Of the following, the food containing a complete protein is

    A. navy beans
    B. almonds
    C. beef round
    D. gelatin

8. The MOST important of the nutritive contributions made by cereals in the diet is their content of

    A. B-complex vitamins
    B. minerals
    C. protein
    D. carbohydrate

9. Loss of vitamin C content during cooking is increased by

    A. excessive stirring
    B. low cooking temperature
    C. low storage temperature
    D. use of a cover on the cooking utensil

10. A research project to improve the world-wide protein deficiency was sponsored recently by

    A. UNICEF
    B. ICNND
    C. India
    D. U.S. Department of Agriculture

11. An individual with coronary heart disease should

    A. keep the fat intake low
    B. have a high cholesterol intake
    C. eat only hydrogenated fats
    D. have a medium to high sodium intake

12. Vitamin A is

    A. water-soluble
    B. a precursor of carotene
    C. useful in preventing rickets
    D. fat-soluble

13. The vitamin A value of carrots is HIGHEST when the carrots are

    A. harvested young as baby carrots
    B. grown in rich loam
    C. mature, of at least 2" crown diameter
    D. cooked in boiling salted water

14. Loss of nutrients in frozen vegetables frequently occurs when they are

    A. frozen whole   B. dehydro frozen
    C. blanched   D. sliced or chopped

15. Which of the following foods contains the calcium equivalent to that in one glass of milk?

    A. One-third cup evaporated milk
    B. Three ounces American cheese
    C. One-half cup turnip greens
    D. One dozen soft shelled clams

16. Which of the following vitamins is NOT water soluble?

    A. Vitamin C   B. Thiamin
    C. Niacin   D. Vitamin D

17. It is recommended that milk not be subjected to direct rays of the sun because it might destroy one of the following nutrients:

    A. Thiamin   B. Niacin
    C. Riboflavin   D. Pyridoxin

18. A two-ounce portion of freshly opened canned juice which will contain the largest amount of ascorbic acid is

    A. lemon   B. grapefruit
    C. tomato   D. orange

19. Baking soda should not be used in vegetable cookery because it

    A. gives a bitter flavor
    B. destroys the chlorophyll
    C. destroys thiamin
    D. destroys vitamin A

20. The toasting of a piece of bread is an example of

    A. gelatinization   B. mastication
    C. carbonation   D. dextrinization

21. A rich source of vitamin K is

    A. butter   B. spinach   C. oranges   D. milk

22. The nutrient losses in the dehydration process are similar to those in

    A. sterilization   B. electronic cooking
    C. evaporation   D. pasteurization

23. A safe daily dietary for a reduction regimen will supply APPROXIMATELY _____ calories.

    A. 2500   B. 1500   C. 2000   D. 3000

24. When a diabetic needing insulin eats more food than his prescribed diet allows, a possible resulting danger is the development of

    A. shock   B. stroke   C. acidosis   D. hemorrhage

25. A good source of riboflavin is

    A. milk   B. onions
    C. vegetable fats   D. orange juice

KEY (CORRECT ANSWERS)

1. A
2. A
3. C
4. A
5. B

6. D
7. C
8. A
9. A
10. A

11. A
12. D
13. C
14. D
15. A

16. D
17. C
18. C
19. D
20. D

21. B
22. D
23. B
24. C
25. A

———

TEST 2

DIRECTIONS: Each question or incomplete statement is followed by several suggested answers or completions. Select the one that BEST answers the question or completes the statement. *PRINT THE LETTER OF THE CORRECT ANSWER IN THE SPACE AT THE RIGHT.*

1. Of the following 100 gram portions of fresh substance, the one which yields the MOST iron is 1.____

    A. beef, all lean
    B. egg yolk
    C. dried beans
    D. dried peas

2. The following foods tend to diminish acidity in the urine: 2.____

    A. Tomatoes, oranges, apricots, pineapple
    B. Tomatoes, cranberries, plums, apricots
    C. Tomatoes, prunes, apricots, pineapple
    D. Cranberries, oranges, apricots, pineapple

3. The vitamin MOST readily destroyed in cooking is 3.____

    A. vitamin A
    B. ascorbic acid
    C. vitamin D
    D. riboflavin

4. The amount of calcium required for a one-year-old child is 4.____

    A. less than is needed by a very active man
    B. as much as is needed by a pregnant woman
    C. more than that needed by a very active woman
    D. more than that needed by a ten-year-old child

5. The bodily requirement of protein needed by a man on a reducing diet is 5.____

    A. less than the amount needed on his normal diet
    B. more than the amount needed on his normal diet
    C. the same amount that is required by an adolescent boy
    D. the same amount that is required on his normal diet

6. When food is taken into the stomach, 6.____

    A. protein food stays longer than carbohydrate
    B. emulsified fats leave first
    C. mixtures of fat and protein are quickly digested
    D. fat leaves before protein

7. Injections of insulin may be needed 7.____

    A. to promote oxidation
    B. to raise the concentration of glucose in the blood
    C. to lower the concentration of glucose in the blood
    D. replace adrenaline

8. *Depot fat* refers to 8.____

A. deposits of body fat as reserve fuel
B. fat the body cannot synthesize
C. fat the body cannot re-form
D. fatty acids and glycerols which cannot be re-synthesized by the body

9. An example of a fatty acid is _____ acid.

   A. ascorbic   B. lactic   C. lauric   D. acetic

10. Although milk is said to be the perfect food, it is particularly deficient in one of the following:

    A. Iron   B. Vitamin C
    C. Vitamin D   D. Sulfur

11. The number of calories yielded by the anabolism of one gram of carbohydrates is

    A. two   B. four   C. six   D. ten

12. Egg yolk is rich in

    A. manganese   B. calcium   C. phosphorus   D. potassium

13. For normal nutrition, the tissues of the body must be in a state of saturation with respect to vitamin

    A. A   B. B   C. C   D. E

14. In nutrition, the utilization of the absorbed products is called

    A. anabolism   B. osmosis
    C. metabolism   D. catabolism

15. The food which will produce an acid ash is

    A. dried beans   B. carrots
    C. rice   D. sweet potatoes

16. Carbohydrates are classified chemically according to the number of

    A. oxides   B. saccharides
    C. hydroxides   D. carbides

17. The MAXIMUM number of hours during which extracted exposed orange juice will retain effective vitamin C content is

    A. 12   B. 24   C. 36   D. 48

18. Irradiation of foods produces vitamin

    A. A   B. B   C. C   D. D

19. Eggs supplement milk because they provide

    A. protein   B. fat   C. iron   D. vitamins

20. The eating of coarse foods helps in

    A. digesting starches   B. digesting proteins
    C. preventing constipation   D. repairing muscles

21. Water is a

    A. regulator of body processes
    B. vitamin-rich food
    C. destroyer of vitamins
    D. fuel food

21._____

22. The energy value of the foodstuffs that oxidize in the body can be measured by

    A. calories
    B. body weight
    C. weight of food
    D. quality of the food

22._____

23. A good breakfast judged according to growth elements contained in the food would be

    A. orange juice, toast, and coffee
    B. bacon, waffles, and syrup
    C. cereal, milk, rolls, and butter
    D. prunes, cereal, toast, and milk

23._____

24. A food that is rich in mineral matter is

    A. white flour
    B. cabbage
    C. butter
    D. ready-to-eat cereals

24._____

25. Nutritionally, the BEST way to serve fruits is to

    A. bake them
    B. serve them raw
    C. steam them
    D. stew them

25._____

KEY (CORRECT ANSWERS)

1.	A	11.	B
2.	A	12.	C
3.	A	13.	C
4.	B	14.	C
5.	B	15.	C
6.	C	16.	B
7.	C	17.	B
8.	A	18.	D
9.	C	19.	C
10.	A	20.	C

21. A
22. A
23. D
24. D
25. B

TEST 3

DIRECTIONS: Each question or incomplete statement is followed by several suggested answers or completions. Select the one that BEST answers the question or completes the statement. *PRINT THE LETTER OF THE CORRECT ANSWER IN THE SPACE AT THE RIGHT.*

1. A rich source of riboflavin is
   A. turnips   B. legumes
   C. whole grains   D. milk and its products

2. To promote normal vision is a function of vitamin
   A. A   B. B   C. C   D. D

3. To stimulate the appetite is the function of vitamin
   A. A   B. B_1 C. C   D. D

4. Proteins are classified according to the contained amount of
   A. oxygen   B. carbon
   C. amino acids   D. purins

5. Rickets is a deficiency disease due to an insufficient supply of vitamin
   A. A   B. B   C. C   D. D

6. Nicotinic acid is used in the treatment of
   A. psoriasis   B. pellagra   C. beri-beri   D. scurvy

7. Cane sugar is
   A. invertase   B. sucrose   C. dextrose   D. levulose

8. Surplus vitamin A is stored in the
   A. kidneys   B. liver   C. blood   D. muscles

9. Fish liver oils are the richest source of vitamin
   A. A   B. B   C. C   D. D

10. Direct irradiation increases the content of vitamin
    A. A   B. B   C. C   D. D

11. The number of calories yielded by the anabolism of one gram of fat is
    A. 6   B. 7   C. 8   D. 9

12. The LEAST expensive simple sugar is
    A. levulose   B. lactose   C. glucose   D. galactose

13. The element that constitutes the major portion of the weight of the human body is
    A. copper   B. sodium   C. calcium   D. iron

14. The development of the disease known as beri-beri is due to a marked deficiency of vita-   14.____
    min

    A. A   B. B   C. B₁   D. C

15. Compared with whole cereals, soybeans have   15.____

    A. equal vitamin A values   B. greater cellulose content
    C. lesser vitamin A values   D. greater vitamin A values

16. A complete protein found in milk is   16.____

    A. gliadin   B. ovalbumin   C. casein   D. albumin

17. Resistance to infection is a function of vitamin   17.____

    A. A   B. B   C. C   D. D

18. A fat-soluble vitamin is   18.____

    A. A
    C. C
    B. B₁
    D. riboflavin

19. The largest percentage of gluten protein is found in   19.____

    A. oats   B. barley   C. rye   D. wheat

20. The body can produce vitamin   20.____

    A. A   B. B   C. C   D. D

21. The food that will produce an alkaline ash is   21.____

    A. oatmeal   B. eggs   C. oysters   D. bananas

22. Compared with the average reported by the Department of Agriculture for whole grain   22.____
    wheat flour, enriched flour contains iron and thiamine _____ average.

    A. exactly at the   B. above the
    C. approximately at   D. below the

23. The nutrients that can be purchased in the fall at lowest cost per pound of such nutrients 23.____
    is

    A. kidney beans   B. oranges
    C. chopped beef   D. flounder

24. The RICHEST food source of vitamin A is   24.____

    A. milk   B. egg yolk
    C. spinach   D. carrots

25. Efficient utilization of both calcium and phosphorus depends on a supply of vitamins   25.____

    A. A, B, E   B. B, D, G   C. A, C, D   D. C, E, G

KEY (CORRECT ANSWERS)

1.	D	11.	D
2.	A	12.	C
3.	B	13.	C
4.	C	14.	B
5.	D	15.	D
6.	B	16.	C
7.	B	17.	A
8.	B	18.	A
9.	D	19.	D
10.	D	20.	D

21. D
22. C
23. A
24. C
25. C

TEST 4

DIRECTIONS: Each question or incomplete statement is followed by several suggested answers or completions. Select the one that BEST answers the question or completes the statement. *PRINT THE LETTER OF THE CORRECT ANSWER IN THE SPACE AT THE RIGHT.*

1. The part of broccoli which is RICHEST in important nutritive content is the   1._____
   A. stem   B. leaf   C. flowerlet   D. root

2. Vitamin loss in cooking frozen non-acid vegetables is MOST commonly due to   2._____
   A. rapid boiling   B. overcooking
   C. leaching   D. oxidation

3. Of the following, the only substance which affects the nutritive value of bread is   3._____
   A. yeast   B. bread softener
   C. mold inhibitor   D. bran

4. The group which contains a foodstuff NOT soluble in water is   4._____
   A. calcium, iron, thiamine, niacin
   B. vitamins B, G, niacin, and C
   C. vitamins A, D, niacin, and E
   D. phosphorus, iron, calcium, iodine

5. *Enriched* flours and breads are wheat products to which have been added specific amounts of thiamin, niacin, and   5._____
   A. iron   B. riboflavin and iron
   C. calcium and iron   D. ascorbic acid and iron

6. A diet of commonly available foodstuffs will furnish a healthy person more than adequate amounts of all the known essential vitamins EXCEPT vitamin   6._____
   A. A   B. B   C. C   D. D

7. Which of the following should NOT be consumed by someone suffering from hypertension due to its naturally high salt content?   7._____
   A. Celery   B. Carrots   C. Rice   D. Bananas

8. A vegetable source of protein food is   8._____
   A. legumes   B. chutney
   C. gelatin   D. Irish moss

9. Of the following, a rich source of the vitamin B complex is   9._____
   A. seafoods   B. refined cereals
   C. citrus fruits   D. whole grains

10. The chemical name for vitamin C is _____ acid.   10._____
    A. cevitamic   B. citric   C. amino   D. lactic

41

11. Substances which promote growth and energy and help the body resist diseases are 11.____
    A. proteins
    B. amino acids
    C. fatty acids
    D. vitamins

12. A ketogenic diet is a diet with a high percentage of 12.____
    A. vitamins   B. fat   C. protein   D. minerals

13. Of the following, the LEAST costly, as well as the BEST source of calcium and phosphorus in a form in which it may be assimilated directly, is 13.____
    A. dried milk
    B. meat
    C. dried fruits and vegetables
    D. multiple-vitamin-mineral preparations

14. The diet of MOST Puerto Ricans is deficient in 14.____
    A. vitamin B and calcium
    B. carbohydrates, proteins, and cellulose
    C. protein, calcium, vitamin A, and riboflavin
    D. fats and carbohydrates

15. Cutting down the amount of cane sugar improves the average diet because sugar tends to 15.____
    A. cause diabetes
    B. stimulate the appetite
    C. cause overweight
    D. irritate the digestive tract

16. According to United States law, the percentage of milk fat by weight which butter MUST contain is not less than 16.____
    A. 75%   B. 80%   C. 65%   D. 90%

17. Iodine is necessary for the normal functioning of the 17.____
    A. red blood cells
    B. thyroid gland
    C. heart
    D. hemoglobin

18. The diet of a 72-year-old woman should include extra quantities of 18.____
    A. proteins
    B. vitamins
    C. minerals
    D. carbohydrates

19. Of the following foods, the one which could be included in a low residue diet is 19.____
    A. applesauce
    B. mashed potatoes
    C. steamed asparagus
    D. creamed celery

20. As an aid in making up the daily quota of calcium and phosphorus, serve 20.____
    A. soda crackers and fruit jelly
    B. pineapple juice to start the dinner
    C. milk puddings as desserts
    D. a peanut butter sandwich at lunch

21. Of the following foods, the RICHEST source of iodine is 21.____

    A. lake trout
    B. corn
    C. oranges
    D. salmon

22. An element found in proteins but NOT found in carbohy-drates is 22.____

    A. nitrogen   B. carbon   C. oxygen   D. hydrogen

23. Foods such as custards, poached eggs, milk, toast, cereals, puddings, and ice cream are served when the prescribed diet is 23.____

    A. bland   B. liquids   C. soft   D. regular

24. Each of the vitamins below is correctly paired with the disease it helps to prevent EXCEPT vitamin 24.____

    A. A - pellagra
    B. B_1 - beri-beri
    C. C - scurvy
    D. D - rickets

25. Of the following, the BEST source of the vitamin which functions to condition the walls of blood vessels is 25.____

    A. carrots
    B. milk
    C. orange juice
    D. whole wheat bread

KEY (CORRECT ANSWERS)

1.	B	11.	D
2.	C	12.	B
3.	A	13.	A
4.	C	14.	C
5.	B	15.	C
6.	D	16.	B
7.	A	17.	B
8.	A	18.	B
9.	D	19.	B
10.	B	20.	C

21. D
22. A
23. C
24. A
25. C

TEST 5

DIRECTIONS: Each question or incomplete statement is followed by several suggested answers or completions. Select the one that BEST answers the question or completes the statement. *PRINT THE LETTER OF THE CORRECT ANSWER IN THE SPACE AT THE RIGHT.*

1. Body weight can be reduced at the rate of about one pound per week by the daily withdrawal from the bodily stores of about _____ calories.   1.____

   A. 500   B. 1000   C. 2000   D. 3000

2. The availability of iron derived from various sources depends on the   2.____

   A. form in which it occurs in the food
   B. supply of thiamin
   C. amount of iron-rich foods provided
   D. amount of iron required by the body

3. All of the following foods furnish approximately 100 calories EXCEPT   3.____

   A. 1 large orange   B. 1 head lettuce
   C. 1 tbsp. butter   D. 5/8 cup whole milk

4. Excess frost on a package of frozen vegetables indicates   4.____

   A. probable loss of vitamin C
   B. inferior packing
   C. inferior produce
   D. poor air circulation in the freezer

5. Caribbean children find it difficult to adjust to the usual foods of New York City because they are not accustomed to   5.____

   A. fresh fruits   B. rice
   C. fresh eggs   D. fresh milk

6. Dehydration of food by sunlight results in   6.____

   A. loss of vitamin C content
   B. increased bulk
   C. increased vitamin D
   D. lower calcium content

7. Of the following, the one which is MOST economical for protein re-enforcement of the diet is   7.____

   A. egg yolk   B. ice cream
   C. cream cheese   D. skim milk powder

8. The riboflavin content of a food is GREATLY lowered by exposure of the food to   8.____

   A. heat   B. freezing temperature
   C. air   D. sunlight

9. The chemical name for *animal starch* is 9.____

   A. glycogen B. glucose
   C. amylodextrin D. dextrose

10. According to the prevailing concept, a diet rich in unsaturated fatty acids can be labeled 10.____

    A. anti-atherogenic B. atherogenic
    C. anti-scorbutic D. nephritic

11. Compared with 16-20 year-old girls, 13-15 year-old girls need 11.____

    A. less iron B. less vitamin D
    C. more calcium D. more protein

12. To provide vitamin C, serve 12.____

    A. apricots B. whole wheat bread
    C. cole slaw D. cocoa

13. Compared with the recommended figure of 50%, the ACTUAL percentage of food calories derived from protective foods in the American diet is 13.____

    A. 20%   B. 25%   C. 33%   D. 45%

14. To provide the basis for building red blood corpuscles, feed 14.____

    A. cream tapioca B. buttered toast
    C. yolk of egg D. white of egg

15. Salt water fish, as compared with fresh water fish, contain more 15.____

    A. iodine   B. calcium   C. copper   D. magnesium

16. As an aid to make up the daily quota of calcium and phosphorus, serve 16.____

    A. water at mealtime
    B. milk puddings as desserts
    C. pineapple juice as an appetizer
    D. peanut butter on white bread

17. Potatoes are superior in nutritive value when 17.____

    A. cut in strips and fried
    B. cut up and boiled
    C. baked whole
    D. boiled whole without skins

18. An EXCELLENT source of fibrous material is 18.____

    A. pureed potato soup B. cream of wheat cereal
    C. mozzarella cheese D. escarole

19. For HIGHEST nutritive value at least cost, of the following choose 19.____

    A. meatloaf, soybeans, and vegetables
    B. round steak with brown rice
    C. meatballs and spaghetti
    D. braised mushrooms and liver steak

20. The extractives in meat are valuable because they   20.____
   A. provide energy
   B. are a source of iron
   C. supply vitamins
   D. aid digestion

21. Whole-grain cereals are preferred because they   21.____
   A. have flavor
   B. are easily prepared
   C. contain vitamins
   D. provide calories

22. The outside leaves of salad greens   22.____
   A. contain more vitamin A and iron
   B. make the salad crispy
   C. are more tender
   D. contain more roughage

23. The BEST dessert to provide additional protein in a meal is   23.____
   A. apple pie
   B. baked custard
   C. fruit jello
   D. apricot whip

24. Vitamin C is present in _____ milk.   24.____
   A. evaporated
   B. pasteurized
   C. raw
   D. condensed

25. The RICHEST vegetable source of riboflavin is   25.____
   A. lima beans
   B. fresh peas
   C. lettuce
   D. dried soybeans

KEY (CORRECT ANSWERS)

1.	A	11.	D
2.	A	12.	A
3.	B	13.	C
4.	A	14.	C
5.	D	15.	A
6.	A	16.	B
7.	D	17.	C
8.	D	18.	D
9.	A	19.	A
10.	A	20.	D

21. C
22. A
23. B
24. C
25. C

EXAMINATION SECTION
TEST 1

DIRECTIONS: Each question or incomplete statement is followed by several suggested answers or completions. Select the one that BEST answers the question or completes the statement. *PRINT THE LETTER OF THE CORRECT ANSWER IN THE SPACE AT THE RIGHT.*

1. In the last fifty years, the proportion of calories from milk, cheese, fruits, and vegetables in the American diet has

    A. remained the same B. doubled
    C. tripled D. quadrupled

2. Interference with absorption of vitamin A may result from

    A. a diet heavy with bulk foods
    B. overconsumption of salad oils
    C. mineral oil in salad dressings
    D. low cholesterol diet

3. Hypoglycemia is a condition of

    A. diseased eyes B. low blood sugar
    C. high blood sugar D. low purin content

4. The term *trace elements* refers to

    A. minerals needed in very small amounts in nutrition
    B. substance which trace circulation in the body
    C. tools used in sewing
    D. potent drugs used as pain killer

5. One of the EARLIEST symptoms of a thiamine deficiency is

    A. polyneuritis B. anorexia
    C. nyctalopia D. conjunctivitis

6. In measuring vitamin A value in foods, the international unit is defined as the activity of

    A. 5.0 mg. calciferol B. 6.0 gm. tocopherol
    C. 6.0 gm. carotene D. 0.6 mcg. betacarotene

7. The RICHEST food sources of folacin are

    A. livers and green leafy vegetables
    B. eggs and milk
    C. cereals
    D. fats

8. Folacin is necessary for

    A. digestion of carbohydrates
    B. metabolism of sterols
    C. synthesis of chlorophyll
    D. hematopoiesis

9. Avidin is a(n)

   A. vitamin   B. protein   C. fiber   D. fabric

10. The liver is the storage depot in the body for vitamin

    A. A   B. E   C. C   D. B

11. The anti-xerophthalmia vitamin is vitamin

    A. A   B. B   C. E   D. K

12. Riboflavin is EASILY destroyed by

    A. alkalies and light
    B. acids and oxygen
    C. heat and agitation
    D. air and agitation

13. The material which destroys the activity of biotin is

    A. the protein found in uncooked egg white
    B. fluorides in drinking water
    C. iodides in medications
    D. fluorescent substances found in milk

14. The diet prescribed in diverticulitis is one that is

    A. high in calorie value
    B. high in roughage content
    C. low residue, bland
    D. high protein, bland

15. In typhoid fever, the diet should be

    A. *high* in calories and residue
    B. *low* in calories, high in residue
    C. *high* in calories, low in residue
    D. *high* in fruit juice content

16. Of the following, the HIGHEST in caloric value is one cupful

    A. strained honey
    B. orange juice
    C. sugar
    D. homogenized milk

17. Among the following, the BEST food source of thiamine is

    A. refined sugars
    B. fats
    C. egg white
    D. pork

18. In the list below, the BEST source of vitamin A is

    A. wheat germ
    B. pork
    C. milk
    D. spinach

19. A disadvantage resulting from the intake of mineral oil is that it

    A. adds calories
    B. reduces weight
    C. impairs the appetite
    D. dissolves vitamin A

20. The MAJOR influence in the decline of endemic goiter in the United States is the use of

    A. saffron oil
    B. homogenized milk
    C. iodized salt
    D. enriched cereals

21. Cretinism is a form of idiocy due to extreme deficiency of secretion by

    A. fat-soluble vitamins in the diet
    B. B-complex vitamins in the diet
    C. thyroid gland
    D. adrenal glands

22. Fuel value of foods is determined by use of a(n)

    A. caloric unit
    B. calorific unit
    C. calciferol
    D. calorimeter

23. For the average American, minerals of value as food supplements for the diet are calcium and

    A. phosphorus, sodium, and choline
    B. chlorine, magnesium, and iron
    C. phosphorus, iron, and iodine
    D. chlorine, iron, and manganese

24. For the average American, the vitamins of value as food supplements are thiamine, pyrodoxine, riboflavin, calciferol, ascorbic acid, and

    A. niacin, B_{12}, A
    B. B_6, B_{12}, folic acid
    C. B_{12}, K, A
    D. B_{12}, A, E

25. Nyctalopia results from a lack of

    A. vitamin A
    B. fluorine
    C. citric acid
    D. flavinoids

KEY (CORRECT ANSWERS)

1. B
2. C
3. B
4. A
5. B
6. D
7. A
8. D
9. B
10. A
11. A
12. A
13. A
14. C
15. C
16. A
17. D
18. D
19. D
20. C
21. C
22. D
23. C
24. A
25. A

TEST 2

DIRECTIONS: Each question or incomplete statement is followed by several suggested answers or completions. Select the one that BEST answers the question or completes the statement. *PRINT THE LETTER OF THE CORRECT ANSWER IN THE SPACE AT THE RIGHT.*

1. The number of amino acids which are essential for human growth is   1.____
   A. 23   B. 8   C. 16   D. 6

2. Of the following statements, the one which expresses a food fallacy is: 2.____
   A. There are no *miracle* foods
   B. Canned foods can be left in their original containers without danger
   C. Vitamin tablets or concentrates are necessary for guarantee of an adequate diet
   D. Toasting a slice of bread will not alter its calorie content

3. The dietary contribution of fish is   3.____
   A. a high concentration of vitamin C
   B. a high concentration of vitamin B_{12}
   C. all the nutrients except carbohydrates
   D. a high concentration of iron

4. A component of vegetable oils and some fish which will increase exertion of bile salts and thus lower cholesterol is   4.____
   A. stearic acid   B. oleic acid
   C. linoleic acid   D. acrolein

5. The vitamin for which dried beans and peas are especially valuable is   5.____
   A. ascorbic acid   B. riboflavin
   C. niacin   D. thiamine

6. Especially notable for vitamin C content are the following: 6.____
   A. Dry beans and peas
   B. Raw cabbage and green peppers
   C. Crisp radishes and corn
   D. Okra and parsnips

7. A deficiency of riboflavin results in   7.____
   A. xerophthalmia   B. polyneuritis
   C. cutaneous lesions   D. chielosis

8. Of the following, the RICHEST source of vitamin E is   8.____
   A. liver   B. green leafy vegetables
   C. wheat germ oil   D. egg yolk

9. Of the following, the number of calories which MOST NEARLY approximates the daily fuel needs of a moderately active 25-year-old woman is   9.____
   A. 1500   B. 2000   C. 2500   D. 3500

50

10. Vitamin A food value is

    A. lacking in yams
    B. fairly constant in dairy products
    C. closely related to green coloring in vegetables
    D. closely related to sun available during growing time

11. The unit of measurement adopted for vitamins and minerals is based on the

    A. minimum daily requirement
    B. recommended dietary allowance
    C. available specific nutrients
    D. regional and cultural food patterns

12. Of the following, the RICHEST source of iron is

    A. citrus fruit   B. cheese
    C. apricots   D. whole wheat

13. The simplified method of calculating diabetic diets is based on

    A. the food exchange plan
    B. substituting orinase for insulin injections
    C. high vitamin content
    D. basic requirements of protein intake

14. When planning diets for diabetic patients, it is recommended that use be made, in proper amounts, of _____ foods.

    A. specialty   B. dietetically canned
    C. natural   D. fatty

15. Of the following fruits, the one which increases acidity in the body is

    A. tomatoes   B. oranges   C. prunes   D. peaches

16. Lipase

    A. controls the blood level of cholesterol
    B. is a polyunsaturated fatty acid
    C. is an enzyme
    D. gives color to green vegetables

17. Of the following, the foods which should be excluded from a minimum residue diet are

    A. milk and milk drinks   B. noodles and macaroni
    C. honey and jelly   D. carbonated beverages

18. Ascorbic acid is the chemical name for

    A. vitamin C   B. vitamin A
    C. a liver extract   D. an iron preparation

19. The real harm resulting from a ready and wide acceptance of food fads is that

    A. nutritional quackery costs several millions of dollars each year
    B. real dietitians and nutritionists lose prestige

C. proper medical attention for the patient is delayed
D. quacks and food faddists benefit

20. Of the following, the foods LOWEST in cholesterol are

    A. homogenized milk and light cream
    B. butter and cheese
    C. fruits and cereals
    D. fruits and cheese

21. Cheese is rich in

    A. calcium   B. potassium   C. iron   D. manganese

22. The anti-hemorrhagic vitamin is

    A. niacin   B. vitamin A
    C. vitamin K   D. riboflavin

23. A complete protein is found in

    A. navy beans   B. peas
    C. lean meat   D. gelatin

24. Butter provides vitamin

    A. G   B. B_1 C. D   D. C

25. The vitamin that is LESS easily destroyed in an acid medium than when the medium is alkaline is

    A. A   B. B   C. C   D. D

KEY (CORRECT ANSWERS)

1.	B	11.	D
2.	C	12.	C
3.	C	13.	A
4.	C	14.	C
5.	D	15.	C
6.	B	16.	C
7.	D	17.	A
8.	C	18.	A
9.	C	19.	C
10.	C	20.	C

21. A
22. C
23. C
24. C
25. C

TEST 3

DIRECTIONS: Each question or incomplete statement is followed by several suggested answers or completions. Select the one that BEST answers the question or completes the statement. *PRINT THE LETTER OF THE CORRECT ANSWER IN THE SPACE AT THE RIGHT.*

1. Proteins of superior quality are
   - A. meats, eggs, milk
   - B. meats, groats, beans
   - C. rice, beans, eggs
   - D. samp, milk, eggs

   1.____

2. Proteins are classified according to the contained amount of
   - A. carbon
   - B. purins
   - C. amino acids
   - D. oxygen

   2.____

3. MOST economic for protein reinforcement of the diet is
   - A. skim milk powder
   - B. egg yolk
   - C. ice cream
   - D. cream cheese

   3.____

4. The addition of sodium bicarbonate when cooking green vegetables
   - A. lowers the boiling point
   - B. improves the taste
   - C. reduces the vitamin content
   - D. inhibits digestion

   4.____

5. Poor diet may influence the occurrence of
   - A. cancer
   - B. apoplexy
   - C. metabolic difficulties
   - D. flow of bile

   5.____

6. Diet therapy is concerned PRINCIPALLY with
   - A. reducing fat intake
   - B. stimulating impaired tissues
   - C. modifying the usual diet of the patient
   - D. increasing protein intake

   6.____

7. The BEST dessert to provide additional protein for a meal is
   - A. apple pie
   - B. fruit jello
   - C. baked custard
   - D. apricot whip

   7.____

8. To assure adequate nutrition for the aged, provide
   - A. excess minerals and vitamins
   - B. a standard general diet
   - C. a 4-year-old child's diet
   - D. adequate quantities of food

   8.____

9. The diet of a 72-year-old obese woman should include extra quantities of
   - A. proteins
   - B. minerals
   - C. vitamins
   - D. carbohydrates

   9.____

10. Carbohydrates are stored in the liver in the form of 10.____

    A. maltose   B. dextrose   C. glycogen   D. glucose

11. The ONLY source of nitrogen in the diet is 11.____

    A. carbohydrates   B. fat
    C. protein   D. minerals

12. Some carbohydrates are necessary in a diabetic diet in order that 12.____

    A. sugars may be avoided
    B. fats may be oxidized
    C. loss of weight may be prevented
    D. intestinal putrefaction may be reduced

13. A food that is HIGH in essential fatty acids is 13.____

    A. heavy cream   B. halibut
    C. duck   D. salmon

14. The caloric value of proteins per gram is 14.____

    A. 4   B. 3   C. 6   D. 9

15. Low sodium diets are used for 15.____

    A. prevention of edema
    B. treatment of diabetes
    C. reduction of cholesterol in the blood
    D. treatment of bacterial endocarditis

16. The rice diet useful in the treatment of hypertensive vascular disease is known by the name of 16.____

    A. Kempner   B. Flexner   C. Fleming   D. Harding

17. Pasteurization of milk 17.____

    A. reduces the ascorbic acid content
    B. increases the ascorbic acid content
    C. destroys all bacteria
    D. decreases digestibility

18. Among the following, the group of foods which leave an acid ash in the body is 18.____

    A. meats, fish, poultry   B. fruits, milk, vegetables
    C. green vegetables, sugars   D. pastries, fats, fruits

19. The rate of oxidation of ascorbic acid is reduced by 19.____

    A. heat   B. cold
    C. solution with an alkali   D. exposure to light

20. The diet which emphasizes frequent small feedings of milk and cream alternating with alkaline powders is called the 20.____

    A. Banting   B. Meniere
    C. Sippy   D. anti-atherogenic

21. Vitamin A is contained in

    A. animal tissues and in green yellow vegetables
    B. animal tissues and in plants
    C. plants containing carotene
    D. animal tissues

22. Commonly lacking in the diet of teenage girls are

    A. sodium and copper
    B. vitamin B_{12} and D
    C. iron and calcium
    D. vitamin B_1 and riboflavin

23. Low in unsaturated fats is

    A. olive oil
    B. soybean oil
    C. tallow
    D. cottonseed oil

24. A member of the B-complex which promotes iron metabolism is

    A. thiamine
    B. folic acid
    C. niacin
    D. pyridoxin

25. Reduction in incidence of nausea and vomiting during pregnancy has been ascribed to an increase in

    A. B-complex vitamins
    B. ascorbic acid
    C. vitamin D
    D. minerals

KEY (CORRECT ANSWERS)

1.	A	11.	C
2.	C	12.	B
3.	A	13.	C
4.	C	14.	A
5.	C	15.	A
6.	C	16.	A
7.	C	17.	A
8.	C	18.	A
9.	C	19.	B
10.	C	20.	C

21. C
22. C
23. C
24. B
25. A

TEST 4

DIRECTIONS: Each question or incomplete statement is followed by several suggested answers or completions. Select the one that BEST answers the question or completes the statement. *PRINT THE LETTER OF THE CORRECT ANSWER IN THE SPACE AT THE RIGHT.*

1. The four nutritionally important minerals are iron,

    A. iodine, potassium, and calcium
    B. iodine, phosphorus, and calcium
    C. potassium, phosphorus, and calcium
    D. iodine, sulphur, and calcium

2. Normal peristalsis in the digestive tract is encouraged by

    A. niacin   B. vitamin A
    C. thiamine   D. ascorbic acid

3. A MAIN source of riboflavin is

    A. meat   B. whole grains
    C. fruits and vegetables D. milk

4. Invert sugar is a mixture of equal parts of

    A. lactose and maltose   B. fructose and lactose
    C. fructose and glucose D. maltose and glucose

5. Whole grain products differ from *enriched* products in possessing a greater content of

    A. niacin   B. carbohydrates
    C. riboflavin   D. protein

6. Nutritionists recommend that our yearly per capita intake of sugar be reduced from 100 pounds to

    A. 65   B. 50   C. 35   D. 20

7. Proteins are

    A. capable of precipitating copper in Fehling's solution
    B. chemically insolvent
    C. substitutes for starch in body functions
    D. precursors of body catalysts

8. An inexpensive source of vitamin C is

    A. cabbage   B. asparagus   C. broccoli   D. cucumbers

9. In international units per pound, the United States Department of Agriculture standard for vitamin A fortification of margarine is

    A. 15,000   B. 5,000   C. 9,000   D. 25,000

10. The vitamin C content of 1 cup of pineapple juice is equivalent to that found in _____ cup of orange juice. 10._____

    A. 1   B. 3/4   C. 1/2   D. 1/4

11. Pellagra indicates a deficiency of 11._____

    A. ascorbic acid   B. niacin
    C. thiamine   D. riboflavin

12. Provitamin A is 12._____

    A. ergosterol   B. carotene
    C. lysine   D. pyrodoxine

13. A characteristic of riboflavin deficiency is 13._____

    A. cheilosis   B. catarrh   C. otitis   D. pellagra

14. In anabolism, the number of calories yielded by one gram of carbohydrates is 14._____

    A. two   B. four   C. six   D. eight

15. Cheese is rich in 15._____

    A. calcium   B. iron   C. sodium   D. potassium

16. Whole grain products, in contrast with enriched products, possess more 16._____

    A. hydrocarbons   B. carbohydrates
    C. vitamins   D. proteins

17. The nutritionally important minerals are 17._____

    A. sodium, iodine, potassium, copper
    B. iron, iodine, phosphorus, calcium
    C. iron, potassium, sulphur, copper
    D. sodium, phosphorus, sulphur, calcium

18. Contributing MOST to the weight of the living human body is 18._____

    A. copper   B. sodium   C. calcium   D. iron

19. The item that acts as a catalytic agent for the assimilation of calcium and phosphorus is 19._____

    A. vitamin D   B. fat
    C. vitamin C   D. protein

20. RICHEST vitamin D food for a one-year-old child is 20._____

    A. egg yolk   B. homogenized milk
    C. spinach   D. cod liver oil

21. Vitamin A is used in the body to 21._____

    A. stimulate the appetite   B. maintain nerve tissue
    C. resist infection   D. grow bone

22. Vitamin A is MOST concentrated in

   A. cream
   B. whole milk
   C. skim milk
   D. certified milk

23. HIGHEST in vitamin C is

   A. egg yolk
   B. soft-cooked egg
   C. beef juice
   D. tomato juice

24. Vitamins are lacking in

   A. butter   B. fruit   C. egg   D. sugar

25. The oil RICHEST in vitamin D is

   A. mineral oil
   B. olive oil
   C. crisco
   D. cod liver oil

KEY (CORRECT ANSWERS)

1.	C	11.	B
2.	C	12.	B
3.	D	13.	A
4.	C	14.	B
5.	A	15.	A
6.	B	16.	D
7.	D	17.	B
8.	A	18.	C
9.	A	19.	A
10.	C	20.	D

21. C
22. A
23. D
24. D
25. D

TEST 5

DIRECTIONS: Each question or incomplete statement is followed by several suggested answers or completions. Select the one that BEST answers the question or completes the statement. *PRINT THE LETTER OF THE CORRECT ANSWER IN THE SPACE AT THE RIGHT.*

1. To increase vitamin A in the diet, eat　　　　　　　　　　　　　　　　1._____

    A. cream cheese with chopped nuts on whole wheat toast
    B. tuna fish and celery on enriched white toast
    C. chicken and celery on rye bread
    D. shredded carrot and pineapple on white bread

2. Of the following, the process which adds NO food value to milk is　　　2._____

    A. irradiation　　　　　　　　　　　B. condensation with sugar
    C. fortification　　　　　　　　　　D. homogenization

3. Hot, home-prepared cereals, as compared with dry cereals,　　　　　　3._____

    A. provide more energy　　　　　　　B. cost less
    C. contain more minerals　　　　　　D. contain more vitamins

4. Puréed fruits and vegetables are served during convalescence because they　　4._____

    A. require no chewing
    B. are highly nutritive
    C. do not irritate the digestive tract
    D. appeal to the appetite

5. Of the following, the BEST for growth and general health is　　　　　　5._____

    A. orange juice, oatmeal, buttered toast, coffee
    B. roll with butter, eggs, coffee
    C. cornflakes, fried eggs, muffins, milk
    D. pancakes, syrup, bacon, milk

6. In wheat, the vitamin B complex is in the　　　　　　　　　　　　　　6._____

    A. endosperm　　　　　　　　　　　B. aleuron layer
    C. bran　　　　　　　　　　　　　　D. germ

7. The duration of infectious colds has been materially diminished by dosages of vitamin　　7._____

    A. A　　　　B. B_1　　　　C. B2　　　　D. E

8. A MAJOR source of riboflavin is　　　　　　　　　　　　　　　　　　8._____

    A. meat　　　　　　　　　　　　　　B. whole grains
    C. fruits　　　　　　　　　　　　　　D. milk

9. Rich in thiamine is　　　　　　　　　　　　　　　　　　　　　　　　9._____

    A. orange juice　　　　　　　　　　B. cheese
    C. polished rice　　　　　　　　　　D. brewer's yeast

10. The antihemorrhagic is

    A. riboflavin B. vitamin A
    C. vitamin K D. niacin

11. Anemia responds to

    A. ascorbic acid B. folic acid
    C. niacin D. carotene

12. Legumes and nuts provide much

    A. thiamine B. calcium C. niacin D. sodium

13. MOST of the body's vitamin A is in the

    A. lungs B. kidneys C. liver D. muscles

14. A food rich in vitamin C is

    A. plums B. celery
    C. green pepper D. watermelon

15. The duration of infectious colds has been measurably diminished by administering additional amounts of vitamin

    A. A B. B_1 C. B_2 D. E

16. Carbohydrate stored in the liver is

    A. galleass B. glycogen C. heptarch D. galactose

17. A quart of milk provides an amount of riboflavin equal to that supplied by lean meat weighing _____ pound(s).

    A. 1/2 B. 1 C. 2 D. 3

18. Provitamin A is

    A. ergosterol B. carotene
    C. lysine D. pyrodoxine

19. A person's weight stays the same if he

    A. eats only enough to supply the energy he uses
    B. exercises daily
    C. rests more
    D. eats more fruits and vegetables

20. Enriched white flour contains

    A. niacin, thiamine, and iron
    B. ascorbic acid and vitamin D
    C. vitamin A and niacinamide
    D. folic acid

21. Pellagra is caused by

    A. bacteria B. deficiency of niacin
    C. deficiency of iron D. a virus

22. To preserve vitamin C in cooking frozen vegetables,

    A. cook before thawing in a small amount of boiling water
    B. thaw first and cook quickly
    C. thaw and cook in a small amount of water
    D. keep just below boiling point

23. Calcium and phosphorus are catalytic agents for use of

    A. vitamin D   B. fat
    C. vitamin C   D. protein

24. Thiamine is found in

    A. macaroni   B. rice   C. pork   D. suet

25. The PRINCIPAL food source of calcium is

    A. meats   B. nuts
    C. milk and milk products   D. vegetables

KEY (CORRECT ANSWERS)

1.	D	11.	B
2.	D	12.	A
3.	B	13.	C
4.	C	14.	C
5.	A	15.	A
6.	D	16.	B
7.	A	17.	C
8.	D	18.	B
9.	D	19.	A
10.	C	20.	A

21. B
22. A
23. A
24. C
25. C

EXAMINATION SECTION
TEST 1

DIRECTIONS: Each question or incomplete statement is followed by several suggested answers or completions. Select the one that BEST answers the question or completes the statement. *PRINT THE LETTER OF THE CORRECT ANSWER IN THE SPACE AT THE RIGHT.*

1. If you thoroughly cook your food and eat it promptly, you cannot get food poisoning.   1.____

   A. True   B. False

2. Which of the following long-term complications can result from food poisoning?   2.____

   A. Rheumatoid arthritis   B. Kidney disease
   C. Nerve damage   D. All of the above
   E. None of the above

3. The first symptoms of food poisoning can occur   3.____

   A. immediately
   B. within two to 48 hours after eating
   C. from two days to a week after eating
   D. any of the above

4. You should contact a doctor for possible food poisoning if you experience   4.____

   A. bloody diarrhea or pus in the stool
   B. headache, stiff neck, and fever
   C. diarrhea that has not let up after three days
   D. weakness, numbness, or tingling, usually in the arms or legs but sometimes around the mouth
   E. any of the above

5. Which of these groups has a greater risk of getting food poisoning than the others?   5.____

   A. Smokers
   B. Heavy antacid users
   C. People who drink alcohol at least once a week
   D. Overweight people

6. At least _____ Salmonella bacteria are necessary to give you food poisoning.   6.____

   A. half a dozen   B. one thousand
   C. ten thousand   D. one million

7. Which has been linked to outbreaks of food poisoning caused by E. coli 0157:H7?   7.____

   A. Apple juice   B. Ground beef
   C. Lettuce   D. All of the above

8. More than ten percent of all bottled water starts out as tap water.   8.____

   A. True   B. False

9. An *EPA-approved* water filter meets minimum standards set by the Environmental Protection Agency for removing bacteria and other harmful substances.   9.____

    A. True   B. False

10. To avoid food poisoning from E. coli 0157;H7, cook ground beef until   10.____

    A. the internal temperature reaches 160°F
    B. the juices run clear
    C. no more pink color is evident
    D. all of the above

11. When you cook meat or poultry - or casseroles that contain meat or poultry - what minimum oven temperature should you use?   11.____

    A. 125° F   B. 225° F   C. 325° F   D. 425° F

12. An easy way to reduce the amount of potentially cancer-causing heterocyclic amines (HCAs) that form when chicken is broiled or grilled is to   12.____

    A. keep the chicken refrigerated until just before cooking
    B. remove the skin after the chicken is cooked
    C. remove the skin before the chicken is cooked
    D. before broiling or grilling the chicken, pre-cook it in a microwave for a few minutes and pour off the juices
    E. all of the above

13. Eighty percent of all food poisoning from meat and poultry is caused by   13.____

    A. E. coli 0157:H7
    B. Salmonella and Campylobacter
    C. Staphylococcus
    D. Clostridium

14. Which kind of cutting board is safest for cutting meat and poultry?   14.____

    A. Wood
    B. Plastic
    C. Either, as long as you keep it clean
    D. None of the above

15. Prions are the agents that appear to cause a deadly disease in people who eat meat from cattle with *mad cow disease*. Which cooking method for beef destroys prions?   15.____

    A. Cooking until the internal temperature reaches 180° F
    B. Broiling for at least 15 minutes
    C. Pre-cooking in a microwave for three minutes and pouring off the juices before broiling or grilling
    D. Cooking until no pink color remains and the juices run clear
    E. None of the above

16. It is sale to eat rare hamburgers if the ground beef has been irradiated.   16.____

    A. True   B. False

17. How can you tell if an egg is contaminated with Salmonella? 17.____

    A. The shell is cracked.
    B. The shell has dried chicken feces on it.
    C. The egg has not been kept refrigerated.
    D. You can see a dark spot if you hold the egg up against a light.
    E. You cannot tell.

18. A roasted chicken is thoroughly cooked when the 18.____

    A. thigh reaches an internal temperature of 180°F
    B. juices run clear
    C. leg moves easily in its socket
    D. any of the above

19. Which fish are least likely to contain chemical contaminants like PCBs, mercury, and pesticides? 19.____

    A. Lean ocean fish like cod, flounder, and haddock
    B. Freshwater fish caught in inland lakes like bluefish and lake trout
    C. Farm-raised catfish
    D. Canned tuna

20. More than 90 percent of seafood poisoning cases would be eliminated if people 20.____

    A. bought only government-inspected seafood
    B. cooked their shellfish thoroughly
    C. made sure their seafood was kept on ice until right before it was cooked
    D. only ate fish they caught themselves

21. To avoid excessive exposure to mercury, the Food and Drug Administration recommends that people limit their seafood consumption to an average of 21.____

    A. four ounces a week
    B. two pounds a week
    C. five pounds a week
    D. no limit, as long as most of it is salmon or canned tuna

22. The symptoms of ciguatera, the most common finfish poisoning in the U.S., are 22.____

    A. headache and vomiting
    B. blood in the stool
    C. nausea, cramps, and diarrhea, followed by a *pins and needles* sensation around and inside the mouth and in the hands and feet
    D. any of the above

23. It is safe to eat raw fish as long as it has been marinated in lemon juice or vinegar for at least four hours. 23.____

    A. True   B. False

24. Approximately _____% of fruits and vegetables contains pesticide residues. 24.____

    A. 100   B. 80   C. 50   D. 10

25. Washing fruits and vegetables with special produce washes removes more pesticides than washing them with detergent and water.   25.____

    A. True
    B. False
    C. There is not enough research to tell

26. It is safe to re-freeze food—even meat and poultry—as long as it has been thawed in the refrigerator.   26.____

    A. True   B. False

27. The best way to refrigerate chicken cacciatore that is left over from dinner is in   27.____

    A. several shallow containers
    B. one deep container
    C. the pot in which it was cooked
    D. its original package

28. Once the date stamped on a milk carton has been reached, the milk   28.____

    A. should not be sold
    B. should not be used
    C. has lost most of its nutritional value
    D. all of the above

29. Which warnings does the Food and Drug Administration require on the labels of foods that contain the fake fat olestra (olean)?   29.____

    A. May cause abdominal cramping
    B. May cause loose stools
    C. Inhibits the absorption of some vitamins
    D. Inhibits the absorption of other nutrients
    E. All of the above

30. The safest sweetner to use is   30.____

    A. acesulfame K (Sweet One)
    B. aspartame (NutraSweet or Equal)
    C. saccharin (Sweet 'N Low)
    D. sucralose (Splenda)
    E. sugar or honey

KEY (CORRECT ANSWERS)

1.	B	16.	B
2.	D	17.	E
3.	D	18.	D
4.	E	19.	A
5.	B	20.	B
6.	A	21.	B
7.	D	22.	C
8.	A	23.	B
9.	B	24.	C
10.	A	25.	C
11.	C	26.	A
12.	D	27.	A
13.	B	28.	A
14.	C	29.	E
15.	E	30.	E

SOLUTIONS TO PROBLEMS

1. CORRECT ANSWER: B
   Some bacteria can produce dangerous toxins that are not destroyed even by thorough cooking. What's more, cooked food can become contaminated if it comes in contact with an unwashed utensil, dish, countertop, or hand that was used to prepare tainted uncooked food.

2. CORRECT ANSWER: D
   Salmonella can cause rheumatoid arthritis, E. coli 0157:H7 can cause kidney disease, and Campylobacter or ciguatera (the most common poisoning from finfish) can cause nerve damage.

3. CORRECT ANSWER: D
   Food poisoning is most likely to strike from two hours to two days after eating. But some toxins in fish work within minutes, while botulism could take up to a week.

4. CORRECT ANSWER: E
   Bloody diarrhea or pus in the stool is the classic sign of an E. coli 0157:H7 infection. Headache, stiff neck, plus a fever may be a sign of Listeria monocytogenes infection. Unrelenting diarrhea could lead to life-threatening dehydration. Weakness, numbness, or tingling could be a sign of botulism or food poisoning from tainted seafood.

5. CORRECT ANSWER: B
   Stomach acid helps destroy bacteria, so people who regularly take antacids or drugs like Tagamet or Zantac are more likely to get food poisoning than people who take them sporadically or not at all.

6. CORRECT ANSWER: A
   It does not take much Salmonella to make you ill. The ice cream that made 224,000 people sick in 41 states in 1994 contained only about six Salmonella bacteria in each serving.

7. CORRECT ANSWER: D
   While ground beef is the most common source of E. coli poisoning, apples and lettuce that are contaminated with animal manure also have been linked to outbreaks.

8. CORRECT ANSWER: A
   More than 10 percent of all bottled water started its journey to your glass from some tap. Of course, that does not mean it is more or less likely to contain contaminants.

9. CORRECT ANSWER: B
   No federal agency approves water-treatment units. But filters that use silver must register with the Environmental Protection Agency (EPA). That is all the *approval* means.

10. CORRECT ANSWER: A
    E. coli is destroyed at 160° F, and the only way to be certain is to use a quick-reading thermometer. New research suggests that when the pink color disappears and the juices run clear, the meat may still not be hot enough to kill E. coli.

7 (#1)

11. CORRECT ANSWER: C
Never cook dishes that contain meat or poultry at less than 325° F. At oven temperatures below 325° F, the internal temperature of the food can take too long to reach 140° F. That is the top of what the U.S. Department of Agriculture calls the *Danger Zone*. Below 140° F, any bacteria can double in number in as little as 20 minutes. And those bacteria can produce toxins that are not killed by heat.

12. CORRECT ANSWER: D
Microwaving chicken for two to five minutes and then discarding the juice can reduce HCAs by 90 percent. Marinating (and discarding the marinade) can also reduce HCAs. HCAs are potentially cancer-causing chemicals created when meat, poultry, and fish are cooked at high temperatures.

13. CORRECT ANSWER: B
Salmonella and Campylobacter cause 80 percent of all food poisoning illnesses - and 75 percent of all deaths - from contaminated meat and poultry. And most of the damage comes from poultry. An estimated one in every four chickens sold in the U.S. is contaminated with Salmonella, and as many as nine in every ten are contaminated with Campylobacter.

14. CORRECT ANSWER: C
Bacteria cling to the surfaces of plastic boards, so they can easily rub off onto food. But plastic is easier to clean. With wooden boards, bacteria are absorbed down into the wood fiber and remain beneath the surface, away from food. But wood is harder to keep clean. The best advice: (1) Keep a separate cutting board for meat and poultry, (2) keep your boards clean (put them in the dishwasher or scrub them regularly with a mild bleach solution), and (3) toss any board that has deep knife scars.

15. CORRECT ANSWER: E
Prions are not destroyed by conventional cooking methods. So far, no cases of mad cow disease have been detected here.

16. CORRECT ANSWER: B
Irradiation does not eliminate the need for careful handling. It kills almost all bacteria, insects, and mold, but not what causes mad cow disease, botulism, or hepatitis. And irradiated meat can always become contaminated in the kitchen if it is placed on a dirty cutting board or plate.

17. CORRECT ANSWER: E
Roughly one out of every 10,000 eggs is contaminated with Salmonella bacteria. And they need not be cracked, soiled, or unrefrigerated. If the ovaries of the hen that laid an egg were contaminated, Salmonella could have gotten into the egg before its shell formed. That is why all raw eggs should be handled as if they were contaminated and should be cooked thoroughly...and why it is no longer safe to lick the batter off the bowl or the spatula or your fingers.

18. CORRECT ANSWER: D
Salmonella and other bacteria are killed when poultry reaches 160° F. If you are cooking a whole chicken, all its meat should be at least 160° F when the thigh reaches 180°F. At that point, the juices run clear and the leg moves easily in its socket. (Ground poultry needs to be cooked to at least 165°F.)

19. CORRECT ANSWER: A
The farther a fish is caught from the site of industrial discharges, the less likely it is to contain chemical residues. And leaner fish tend to be cleaner because many contaminants are stored in the fish's body fat. While farm-raised catfish often contain traces of DDT and canned tuna often contain traces of mercury, the tiny amounts are unlikely to be harmful.

20. CORRECT ANSWER: B
Raw shellfish accounts for more than 90 percent of seafood poisoning cases. The most commom culprit is Norwalk virus, which comes from human sewage. It causes nausea, vomiting, or diarrhea, but most of the 100,000 or so people who are attacked each year recover within a day or two. Vibrio vulni-ficus, a bacterium found mostly in the warm waters of the Gulf of Mexico, is less common. But it still kills about a dozen people a year.

21. CORRECT ANSWER: B
To limit exposure to mercury, the FDA recommends that (1) women of childbearing age eat shark or swordfish no more than once a month, (2) everyone else eat no more than seven ounces of shark or swordfish a week, (3) everyone limit grouper, marlin, and orange roughy to 14 ounces a week, and (4) everyone limit total seafood consumption to no more than about two pounds a week.

22. CORRECT ANSWER: C
In addition to nausea, cramps, diarrhea, and a *pins and needles* sensation, ciguatera victims can experience *temperature reversals*, where hot things feel cold and (more likely) cold things feel hot. Most ciguatera cases occur in Florida, Hawaii, Puerto Rico, the Virgin Islands, and Guam. You are most likely to get it from eating contaminated barracuda, grouper, or red snapper. Most people recover after a few weeks, but one in 20 victims may suffer the aftereffects for two years or more.

23. CORRECT ANSWER: B
Ceviche may taste delicious, but *cooking* by marinating does not kill all the harmful bacteria or parasites that the fish could contain. Neither does cutting up raw fish for sushi.

24. CORRECT ANSWER: C
Some 50 percent of fruits and vegetables tested by the FDA contain pesticide residues. Even worse, most of that 50 percent contains residues of more than one pesticide.

25. CORRECT ANSWER: C
According to a recent study, washing produce with a mixture of water and a mild dishwashing detergent (like Palmolive) -combined with peeling carrots and the skins of fruits like apricots and pears and removing the outer leaves of lettuce and cabbage - eliminated all pesticides in half of the fruits and vegetables that contained residues. So far, there is no good research on whether special fruit-and-vegetable washes work any better.

26. CORRECT ANSWER: A
Forget what your mother told you. It is okay to refreeze meat and poultry that was thawed in the refrigerator. Just do not let the food lie around in the refrigerator for more than a day or two before you refreeze it. And do not expect refrozen food to have the same taste or texture as food that was never frozen.

27. CORRECT ANSWER: A
The idea is to get leftovers cooled down below the USDA's *Danger Zone* (40° F-140° F) as quickly as possible. Shallow containers do that best.

28. CORRECT ANSWER: A
Milk that has reached its expiration is still safe and nutritious, and probably will not go sour for another week or so.

29. CORRECT ANSWER: E
Olean reduces your body's ability to absorb vitamins A, D, E, and K. That is why Procter & Gamble adds those vitamins to Olean. But the fake fat also interferes with the absorption of carotenoids like lutein and lycopene, which may help prevent cancer, stroke, and macular degeneration (the major cause of blindness in the elderly). And P&G does not add carotenoids to Olean. Olean also causes a variety of digestive problems.

30. CORRECT ANSWER: E
You are probably better off with a teaspoon of sugar or honey, though they provide empty calories and promote tooth decay. Acesulfame K and saccharin may slightly increase your risk of cancer. Your best bet in an artificial sweetener is aspartame or sucralose, though aspartame should be better tested.

EXAMINATION SECTION
TEST 1

DIRECTIONS: Each question or incomplete statement is followed by several suggested answers or completions. Select the one that BEST answers the question or completes the statement. *PRINT THE LETTER OF THE CORRECT ANSWER IN THE SPACE AT THE RIGHT.*

1. The one of the following which is the MOST important requirement of a good menu is that it

    A. include a large variety of food
    B. list foods which are well-liked
    C. be printed neatly on a clean menu card
    D. be suited to the purpose for which it is planned

    1.____

2. Of the following, the procedure which is MOST desirable for proper tray service is to

    A. heat all dishes before placing them on the tray
    B. serve hot food hot, and cold food cold
    C. have all patients elevated in order to permit easier swallowing of food
    D. always serve iced water on the tray

    2.____

3. The PROPER position for the knife on the tray is

    A. above the dinner plate
    B. across the bread and butter plate
    C. to the right of the dinner plate
    D. next to the fork

    3.____

4. For attractive tray service, it is MOST advisable to serve harvard beets

    A. on the plate with the meat
    B. in a small side vegetable dish
    C. on a bed of shredded lettuce
    D. with a very thick, heavy sauce

    4.____

5. The kitchen dietitian can work MOST efficiently if her office is located

    A. away from the kitchen, so she can be free from distractions
    B. in a central position where she may view all that happens
    C. at the entrance to the kitchen where she can see people entering and leaving
    D. next to the pantry, so she can see that no unauthorized person enters

    5.____

6. The PRIMARY purpose of keeping records in the dietary department is to

    A. reduce waste in ordering food and supplies
    B. increase consumption of the most nutritious foods
    C. train subordinates in office techniques
    D. maintain statistical records of retail prices

    6.____

7. A budget is BEST described as a(n)

    A. detailed plan for expenditures
    B. schedule for figuring depreciation of equipment over a period of years
    C. order for necessary equipment
    D. periodic accounting for past expenditures

8. Of the following, the CHIEF reason why a refrigerator door should NOT be left open is that the open door will

    A. stop the motor
    B. cause a drop in room temperature
    C. permit the cold air to rise to the top
    D. permit warm air to enter the refrigerator

9. Ovens with thermostatic heat controls should be

    A. kept closed at all times
    B. opened carefully to prevent jarring
    C. checked periodically for accuracy
    D. disconnected when not in use

10. The term *net weight* means MOST NEARLY the

    A. actual weight of an item
    B. weight of the container when empty
    C. combined weight of an item and its container
    D. estimated weight of the container alone

11. In requisitioning food, it is LEAST necessary for a dietitian to

    A. specify the exact quantity desired
    B. secure the signature of the cashier
    C. know the delivery times and order accordingly
    D. know the sizes in which foods are marketed

12. When receiving an order of food, it is INADVISABLE for the dietitian to

    A. check carefully against the order or requisition
    B. see that all fresh foods are weighed and checked in at the receiving room
    C. check for quality as well as quantity of foods delivered
    D. subtract two pounds tare from the weight of each package delivered in an order

13. Assume that, when inspecting a delivery of vegetables, you find a large amount of sorrel mixed in with a bushel of spinach.
    The one of the following actions which it is MOST advisable for you to take is to

    A. sort the spinach and sorrel in cleaning and cook them separately to allow greater variety in the menu
    B. discard the sorrel as waste
    C. call the purchasing office and arrange to return the spinach as unsatisfactory
    D. place the sorrel in the refrigerator and return it to the driver on his next delivery

14. When purchasing iceberg lettuce, it is ADVISABLE to look for lettuce which is   14._____
    A. loosely headed, with soft curly leaves and a yellow heart
    B. tightly headed, elongated, with coarse green leaves
    C. tightly headed, with medium green outside leaves and a pale green heart
    D. loosely headed, with elongated stalk and rugged curly leaves

15. The term *30-40 prunes* is used to describe the   15._____
    A. number of prunes in a box
    B. particular variety of prunes
    C. brand name of prunes
    D. number of prunes in a pound

16. When ordering chocolate liquor, the dietitian should expect to receive a _____ choco-   16._____
    late.
    A. solid piece of   B. semi-liquid
    C. liquid   D. glass jar of

17. Of the following, the BEST reason for discarding the green part of potatoes is that it con-   17._____
    tains a poison known as
    A. cevitamic acid   B. citric acid
    C. solanine   D. trichinae

18. The number of cans that a standard case of #10 canned apples USUALLY contains is   18._____
    A. 6   B. 12   C. 18   D. 24

19. Of the following, the person MOST closely associated with work in the field of infant   19._____
    behavior and feeding is
    A. H. Pollack   B. A. Gesell
    C. E.J. Stieglitz   D. J.F. Freeman

20. Of the following, the person BEST known for work in the field of diabetes is   20._____
    A. N. Jolliffe   B. H. Sherman
    C. R.M. Wilder   D. F. Stern

21. An egg which is strictly fresh will   21._____
    A. float in cold water
    B. have a thin and watery egg white
    C. have a swollen egg yolk which is easily broken
    D. sink in cold water

22. Cocoa and chocolate are rich in   22._____
    A. glycogen   B. gum   C. cellulose   D. starch

23. The percentage of protein that is usually converted into glucose in the body is MOST   23._____
    NEARLY
    A. 49%   B. 58%   C. 67%   D. 78%

24. Of the following vegetables, the one which gives the LARGEST yield, pound for pound, when pureed is 24.____

    A. fresh celery
    B. frozen peas
    C. frozen asparagus
    D. fresh carrots

25. If the composition of two small rib chops is Protein - 21 grams and Fat - 17 grams, the number of calories in the two chops is MOST NEARLY 25.____

    A. 136   B. 200   C. 237   D. 257

KEY (CORRECT ANSWERS)

1. D		11. B	
2. B		12. D	
3. C		13. C	
4. B		14. C	
5. B		15. D	
6. A		16. C	
7. A		17. C	
8. D		18. A	
9. C		19. B	
10. A		20. C	

21. D
22. D
23. B
24. D
25. C

TEST 2

DIRECTIONS: Each question or incomplete statement is followed by several suggested answers or completions. Select the one that BEST answers the question or completes the statement. *PRINT THE LETTER OF THE CORRECT ANSWER IN THE SPACE AT THE RIGHT.*

1. An APPROPRIATE substitute for sucrose for a patient on a low carbohydrate diet is 1.____

    A. saccharin   B. casec   C. lactose   D. protinol

2. Of the following, the vegetables which are high in protein and, therefore, sometimes substituted for meat are 2.____

    A. green leafy vegetables   B. legumes
    C. root vegetables   D. gourds

3. When planning menus, it is *advisable* to use fish at least once a week because it is a GOOD source of 3.____

    A. iron   B. vitamin C   C. zinc   D. iodine

4. Of the following, the one which is a *non-nutritive* beverage is 4.____

    A. clear tea   B. orangeade
    C. oatmeal gruel   D. cream soda

5. Macaroni is *usually* used as a substitute for 5.____

    A. salad   B. meat   C. potato   D. dessert

6. Bread is dextrinized by 6.____

    A. toasting   B. chopping
    C. drying in open air   D. soaking in hot water

7. Baked custard is used on the menu CHIEFLY 7.____

    A. as a source of vitamin C
    B. because of its high protein content
    C. to add color
    D. as a source of starch

8. The one of the following which is a *non-irritating* food is 8.____

    A. cabbage   B. pickles   C. spaghetti   D. celery

9. Leaves of rhubarb and beets, when boiled in an aluminum container, will clean the container because they contain 9.____

    A. sulphuric acid   B. oxalic acid
    C. ammonia   D. alkali

10. When refinishing a refrigerator ice cube tray, the one of the following which should NOT be used as a coating material is 10.____

    A. aluminum   B. cadmium   C. tin   D. nickel

11. The Department of Health requires the sterilization of eating utensils by

    A. hot air sterilizers
    B. ultraviolet rays
    C. chemical solutions
    D. water at 180° F

12. Suppose that the dishwashing machine has become clogged with food particles. Of the following, the action which would be MOST advisable for the dietitian to take *first* is to

    A. call the service man to disassemble and clean the machine
    B. instruct the employees assigned to washing dishes about proper scraping of dishes
    C. order the employees to prerinse all dishes in order to prevent clogging
    D. remove the strainer tray

13. The one of the following which is the MOST effective way to rid a food storeroom of mice is to

    A. cement tight all holes which permit invasion
    B. set traps to catch the mice
    C. spread poison around the floor
    D. burn a sulphur candle in the storeroom

14. Black stoves are cleaned BEST by

    A. polishing with an oiled cloth
    B. rubbing with a piece of wax paper
    C. scrubbing with soap and water
    D. heating until they are red hot

15. Of the following, the BEST procedure for cleaning a red quarry tile floor in a hospital kitchen is to

    A. scrub it, then wax the floor
    B. hose it down with steam
    C. wash it with a strong soap
    D. wash it with a lye

16. After making ice cream, it is MOST important that the machine be

    A. rinsed thoroughly in cold water
    B. sterilized
    C. soaked in soap solution
    D. scrubbed with a brush

17. A dietitian assigned to work with clinic patients should have a basic knowledge of the foods of foreign-born people.
    Of the following, the MOST important reason for this is that

    A. it is interesting and exciting to eat the exotic dishes of foreign lands
    B. such knowledge would prove beyond doubt that poor diet is the cause of poor health among the foreign-born

C. such knowledge would help the dietitian to plan the patient's prescribed diet around familiar foods
D. many foreign dishes are more nutritious than American foods

18. The clinic dietitian meets several problems of the aging. The one of the following for which she is LEAST responsible is the

    A. detection of the onset of chronic degenerative diseases
    B. conservation of the health of the individual
    C. re-evaluation of the caloric requirements of aged patients
    D. overcoming of superstitions and food fallacies

19. When advising on methods of economizing, the clinic dietitian should instruct patients to AVOID buying

    A. foods in quantity, even though storage space permits
    B. foods that are in season and in abundance on the market
    C. less expensive cuts of meat
    D. butter, since there are less expensive substitutes on the market

20. The one of the following services which is the LEAST basic function of a nutrition clinic is to

    A. serve as a teaching center for students
    B. provide educational programs for patients of all ages
    C. follow up the nutritional status of individual patients
    D. secure diet histories of patients for the correction of undesirable food habits

21. Time and motion studies in the field of dietetics are used PRIMARILY to

    A. check on lateness and absence records of employees
    B. reduce effort and increase efficiency in performing particular tasks
    C. prepare estimates of time required between requisition and delivery dates
    D. schedule the daily work assignments for the entire staff

22. The PRIMARY purpose of using standardized recipes is to

    A. aid in controlling food costs
    B. encourage the cooks to try out new foods
    C. prepare large quantities of food
    D. determine the caloric values of foods

23. The CHIEF advantage of keeping a perpetual inventory of stock items is that

    A. supplies may be stored more easily
    B. there will be less breakage and loss of stock
    C. it makes it unnecessary to order replacements for stock supplies
    D. the balance on hand at any time is easily determined

24. In order to prevent the loss of vitamins in cooking, it is HOST advisable to

    A. cover the food completely with water while cooking and boil it rapidly
    B. peel and soak vegetables in cold water before cooking

C. dice vegetables into small pieces and boil them in an open pot
D. cook vegetables in the shortest possible time in a covered pot containing little water

25. To marinate is to 25.____
    A. let foods stand in a specially prepared liquid to add flavor or to tenderize them
    B. cook food in liquid just below the boiling point
    C. moisten food while cooking by pouring over it drippings or other liquids
    D. cook food in water at boiling temperature

KEY (CORRECT ANSWERS)

1. A
2. B
3. D
4. A
5. C

6. A
7. B
8. C
9. B
10. B

11. D
12. A
13. A
14. C
15. B

16. B
17. C
18. A
19. D
20. A

21. B
22. A
23. D
24. D
25. A

EXAMINATION SECTION
TEST 1

DIRECTIONS: Each question or incomplete statement is followed by several suggested answers or completions. Select the one that BEST answers the question or completes the statement. *PRINT THE LETTER OF THE CORRECT ANSWER IN THE SPACE AT THE RIGHT.*

1. Spinach should be cooked

    A. in boiling water, without a cover
    B. dry, in an open pot
    C. dry, in a covered pot
    D. in boiling water with a cover

2. For cookies, one may use melted _____ fat.

    A. beef   B. ham   C. chicken   D. lamb

3. Baking powder is used in proportion to the

    A. flour   B. egg   C. liquid   D. shortening

4. To prevent curdling of soft custard, cook

    A. over boiling water
    B. and stir constantly
    C. over a low flame
    D. over water about to boil

5. In dressings, an example of a *permanent emulsion* is

    A. French dressing
    B. mineral oil
    C. mayonnaise dressing
    D. olive oil

6. Eggs stored in the home should be

    A. uncovered in the refrigerator
    B. washed
    C. in a cool place but not in the refrigerator
    D. in a refrigerator in a covered container

7. Meat should be stored in the refrigerator overnight for use on the next day

    A. loosely covered with patapar in the freezing unit
    B. tightly covered with aluminum foil in a cool part
    C. covered with aluminum foil in the freezing unit
    D. loosely covered with wax paper in a cool part

8. The MOST tender cuts of beef come from the

    A. loin and rib
    B. leg and rib
    C. shoulder and loin
    D. rump and neck

9. To preserve vitamin C in cooking frozen vegetables,

    A. cook before thawing in a small amount of boiling water
    B. thaw first and cook quickly

1.____

2.____

3.____

4.____

5.____

6.____

7.____

8.____

9.____

81

C. thaw and cook in a small amount of water
D. keep just below boiling point

10. Calcium and phosphorus are catalytic agents for use of

   A. vitamin D   B. fat   C. vitamin B   D. protein

11. Yeast plants grow BEST at a temperature of _____ F.

   A. 70°-75°   B. 80°-85°   C. 90°-95°   D. 100°-105°

12. Tunnels in plain muffins are due to

   A. overheating
   B. underbeating
   C. using too much shortening
   D. using too little shortening

13. For each cup of sour milk in a recipe, add soda in the amount of _____ teaspoon(s).

   A. 2   B. 1   C. 1/2   D. 1/4

14. Incompletely cooked pork, if eaten, may result in

   A. botulism   B. ptomaine
   C. trichinosis   D. typhoid

15. In cooked frostings, cream of tartar is added to

   A. provide a tang
   B. accelerate crystallization
   C. minimize the size of crystals
   D. increase viscosity

16. When substituting sodium aluminum sulphate-phosphate baking powder in a recipe calling for a tartrate baking powder, use _____ of the former per cup of flour

   A. one-half as much   B. one-half more
   C. the same amount   D. one-quarter

17. The MOST appropriate poultry to buy for a chicken fricassee is the

   A. broiler   B. guinea hen
   C. capon   D. fowl

18. Artichokes are scarce because they

   A. are in slight demand   B. are difficult to digest
   C. do not keep well   D. require special cultivation

19. Less tender cuts of meat may be tenderized by

   A. quick cooking   B. the addition of tomatoes
   C. pan frying   D. broiling

20. The official grades for canned fruits which have been set up by the U.S. Department of Agriculture are A, (Fancy);

A. B, (Choice); C, (Standard)
B. B, (Choice)
C. B, (Choice); C, (Substandard)
D. C, (Standard)

21. If both starch and egg are used for thickening a mixture, the egg should be

    A. thoroughly beaten before it is added to the mixture
    B. added to the mixture after the starch is thoroughly cooked
    C. combined with the liquid ingredients
    D. combined with the dry ingredients

22. For everyday use, it is BEST to maintain the temperature of the refrigerator at _____ F.

    A. 20°-25°   B. 35°-40°   C. 45°-50°   D. 55°-60°

23. As to pork, the federal meat inspection law should be amended to require examination for

    A. botulism   B. trichina   C. tetanus   D. fastigium

24. When all-purpose flour is used in a recipe calling for pastry flour, for each cup of flour in the recipe _____ tablespoonsful.

    A. add two   B. subtract two
    C. add one   D. subtract one

25. Federal law regulates foods sold in

    A. cities   B. rural areas
    C. states   D. interstate commerce

KEY (CORRECT ANSWERS)

1. D   11. D
2. C   12. A
3. A   13. C
4. B   14. C
5. C   15. C

6. D   16. A
7. C   17. A
8. A   18. D
9. A   19. B
10. A   20. A

21. B
22. B
23. B
24. B
25. D

TEST 2

DIRECTIONS: Each question or incomplete statement is followed by several suggested answers or completions. Select the one that BEST answers the question or completes the statement. *PRINT THE LETTER OF THE CORRECT ANSWER IN THE SPACE AT THE RIGHT.*

1. Goiters are caused by lack of

    A. iodine in the food
    B. iron in food
    C. chlorine in the water supply
    D. vitamins in vegetables

    1.____

2. Of the following, the MOST inexpensive source of nutritive food is

    A. soybean   B. cereal   C. eggs   D. meats

    2.____

3. In international units per pound, the vitamin A level of butter is *approximately*

    A. 9,000   B. 15,000   C. 3,000   D. 5,000

    3.____

4. Vitamin A value of carrots is HIGHEST when they are

    A. harvested as baby carrots
    B. harvested later as mature carrots
    C. selected on the basis of variety
    D. planted in rich loam

    4.____

5. Calciferol and viosterol are produced by irradiation of

    A. ergosterol   B. cholesterol
    C. ascorbic acid   D. leucosin

    5.____

6. Provitamin A is

    A. ergosterol   B. carotene
    C. lysine   D. pyrodoxine

    6.____

7. Breast feeding

    A. is unimportant
    B. is a drain on the mother
    C. increases infant development
    D. provides temporary immunity

    7.____

8. A roast shrinks LEAST if

    A. cooked at 300° - 350° F.
    B. first seared
    C. cooked at 500° F.
    D. cooked in a small amount of water

    8.____

9. When making yeast rolls, the milk is scalded in order to

   A. improve the flavor of the product
   B. reduce the size of the air holes
   C. destroy microorganisms
   D. encourage the development of yeast

10. When making medium white sauce, the ratio of fat to flour per cup of milk is

    A. 1 tsp. to 1 tsp.
    B. 2 tbsp. to 2 tbsp.
    C. 1 tbsp, to 1 tbsp.
    D. 1 tbsp. to 2 tbsp.

11. The four nutritionally important minerals are iron,

    A. iodine, potassium, and calcium
    B. iodine, phosphorus, and calcium
    C. potassium, phosphorus, and calcium
    D. iodine, sulphur, and calcium

12. Normal peristalsis in the digestive tract is encouraged by

    A. niacin
    B. vitamin A
    C. thiamine
    D. ascorbic acid

13. A MAIN source of riboflavin is

    A. meat
    B. whole grains
    C. fruits and vegetables
    D. milk

14. Invert sugar is a mixture of equal parts of

    A. lactose and maltose
    B. fructose and lactose
    C. fructose and glucose
    D. maltose and glucose

15. Whole grain products differ from *enriched* products in possessing a GREATER content of

    A. niacin
    B. carbohydrates
    C. riboflavin
    D. protein

16. Nutritionists recommend that our yearly per capita intake of sugar be reduced from 100 pounds to

    A. 65   B. 50   C. 35   D. 20

17. Proteins are

    A. capable of precipitating copper in Fehling's solution
    B. chemically insolvent
    C. substitutes for starch in body functions
    D. precursors of body catalysts

18. An inexpensive source of vitamin C is

    A. cabbage   B. asparagus   C. broccoli   D. cucumbers

19. In international units per pound, the U.S. Department of Agriculture standard for vitamin A fortification of margarine is

    A. 15,000   B. 5,000   C. 9,000   D. 25,000

20. The vitamin C content of one cup of pineapple juice is equivalent to that found in _____ cup of orange juice.

    A. 1 B. 3/4 C. 1/2 D. 1/4

21. Pellagra indicates a deficiency of

    A. ascorbic acid B. niacin
    C. thiamine D. riboflavin

22. A growing child should NOT drink coffee because it

    A. acts as a stimulant B. is habit-forming
    C. reduces milk intake D. spoils the appetite

23. The PRINCIPAL food source of calcium is

    A. meats B. nuts
    C. milk and milk products D. vegetables

24. Legumes and nuts provide a RICH source of

    A. thiamine B. calcium C. niacin D. sodium

25. Since 1850, the per capita consumption of sugar in the United States has increased

    A. 900% B. 150% C. 500% D. 300%

KEY (CORRECT ANSWERS)

1. A 11. C
2. A 12. C
3. B 13. D
4. A 14. C
5. A 15. A

6. B 16. B
7. C 17. D
8. A 18. A
9. B 19. A
10. B 20. C

21. B
22. C
23. C
24. A
25. D

EXAMINATION SECTION
TEST 1

DIRECTIONS: Each question or incomplete statement is followed by several suggested answers or completions. Select the one that BEST answers the question or completes the statement. *PRINT THE LETTER OF THE CORRECT ANSWER IN THE SPACE AT THE RIGHT.*

1. The item that acts as a catalytic agent for the assimilation of calcium and phosphorus is   1.____

    A. vitamin D   B. fat   C. vitamin B   D. protein

2. Contributing MOST to the weight of the living human body is   2.____

    A. copper   B. sodium   C. calcium   D. iron

3. Before cooking, the vegetable that MUST be soaked in water is   3.____

    A. string beans
    B. Brussels sprouts
    C. turnips
    D. celery

4. Amino acids are absorbed MAINLY in the   4.____

    A. stomach   B. liver   C. pancreas   D. intestine

5. Little spoilage occurs in stored, sun-dried fruits because the   5.____

    A. microorganisms have been destroyed
    B. moisture content is low
    C. pectin is inactive
    D. yeasts do not flourish in the absence of light

6. In pickling, the concentrated brine   6.____

    A. softens the cellulose
    B. preserves the original color
    C. retards the growth of microorganisms
    D. increases the acid content

7. Cheese is rich in   7.____

    A. calcium   B. iron   C. sodium   D. potassium

8. Tenderized dried fruits have been   8.____

    A. sulphurized, dried, then partially cooked
    B. dried, partially cooked, then partially dried
    C. partially cooked, dried, then partially cooked
    D. dried, sulphurized, then partially cooked

9. The MOST tender cuts of beef are from the   9.____

    A. loin and rib
    B. leg and rib
    C. shoulder and loin
    D. rump and neck

10. In anabolism, the number of calories yielded by one gram of carbohydrates is

    A. two   B. four   C. six   D. eight

11. When making yeast rolls, the milk is scalded to

    A. improve the flavor of the product
    B. reduce the size of the air holes
    C. destroy the microorganisms
    D. encourage development of the yeast

12. Deterioration of dried vegetables is retarded by

    A. marinating before drying
    B. storage in metal boxes
    C. pre-cooking before drying
    D. infra-red light treatment before packaging

13. The LARGEST percentage of gluten is found in flour made from

    A. rye   B. barley   C. oats   D. wheat

14. A bed roll is a support for the patient's

    A. head   B. knees   C. back   D. feet

15. One pound of dried eggs is equivalent to _____ eggs.

    A. 50-60   B. 30-40   C. 20-25   D. 15-18

16. To store eggs at home,

    A. keep them exposed on the cupboard
    B. wash and place them in the refrigerator
    C. do not wash and place them in the refrigerator
    D. place them in a moderately cool place

17. Disease is MOST commonly spread through

    A. clothing   B. dishes   C. food   D. contact

18. For everyday use, the Fahrenheit temperature of the refrigerator should be

    A. 20°-25°   B. 35°-40°   C. 45°-50°   D. 55°-60°

19. To retard spoilage of bread, baking companies may add sodium

    A. benzoate   B. propionate
    C. sulphathionate   D. hypophosphate

20. Essential to jelly-making is

    A. proto-pectin   B. pectin
    C. pectic acid   D. pectoral liquor

KEY (CORRECT ANSWERS)

1.	A	11.	D
2.	C	12.	C
3.	B	13.	D
4.	D	14.	B
5.	B	15.	B
6.	C	16.	C
7.	A	17.	D
8.	B	18.	B
9.	A	19.	B
10.	B	20.	B

TEST 2

DIRECTIONS: Each question or incomplete statement is followed by several suggested answers or completions. Select the one that BEST answers the question or completes the statement. *PRINT THE LETTER OF THE CORRECT ANSWER IN THE SPACE AT THE RIGHT.*

1. A MAJOR source of riboflavin is

    A. meat
    B. whole grains
    C. fruits
    D. milk

2. In wheat, the vitamin B complex is in the

    A. endosperm
    B. aleuron layer
    C. bran
    D. germ

3. The duration of infectious colds has been materially diminished by dosages of vitamin

    A. A
    B. B_1
    C. B_2
    D. E

4. Yeast plants grow BEST at the Fahrenheit temperature of

    A. 70°-75°
    B. 80°-85°
    C. 90°-95°
    D. 100°-105°

5. A characteristic of riboflavin deficiency is

    A. cheilosis
    B. catarrh
    C. otitis
    D. pellagra

6. Anemia responds to

    A. ascorbic acid
    B. folic acid
    C. niacin
    D. carotene

7. Legumes and nuts provide much

    A. thiamine
    B. calcium
    C. niacin
    D. sodium

8. Rich in thiamine is

    A. orange juice
    B. cheese
    C. polished rice
    D. brewer's yeast

9. Carbohydrate stored in the liver is

    A. galleasss
    B. glycogen
    C. liepstarch
    D. galactose

10. The antihemmorhagic is

    A. riboflavin
    B. vitamin A
    C. vitamin K
    D. niacin

11. At the end of one year, the weight of an infant in relation to its birth weight should be

    A. an increase of 12 oz. monthly
    B. double
    C. 20 pounds more
    D. triple

2 (#2)

12. Pellagra indicates a deficiency of   12.____

    A. ascorbic acid   B. niacin
    C. thiamine   D. riboflavin

13. Provitamin A is   13.____

    A. ergosterol   B. carotene
    C. lysine   D. pyrodoxine

14. The nutritionally important minerals are   14.____

    A. sodium, iodine, potassium, copper
    B. iron, iodine, phosphorus, calcium
    C. iron, potassium, sulphur, copper
    D. sodium, phosphorus, sulphur, calcium

15. Root vegetables are BEST stored in atmosphere that is maintained   15.____

    A. at 36° F   B. dehumidified
    C. at 30° F   D. at 75% humidity

16. The government stamp on meats indicates   16.____

    A. date when slaughtered   B. point of origin
    C. nutritional value   D. quality

17. Whole grain products, in contrast with enriched products, possess more   17.____

    A. hydrocarbons   B. carbohydrates
    C. vitamins   D. proteins

18. In anabolism, the number of calories yielded by one gram of hydrocarbon is   18.____

    A. six   B. seven   C. eight   D. nine

19. In the digestion of starch, the intermediate product is   19.____

    A. dextrin   B. fibrinogen   C. cerine   D. maltine

20. Egg whites whip more quickly at the Fahrenheit temperature of   20.____

    A. 0°   B. 30°   C. 70°   D. 85°

KEY (CORRECT ANSWERS)

1.	D	11.	D
2.	D	12.	B
3.	A	13.	B
4.	B	14.	B
5.	A	15.	A
6.	B	16.	D
7.	A	17.	D
8.	D	18.	D
9.	B	19.	A
10.	C	20.	C

EXAMINATION SECTION
TEST 1

DIRECTIONS: Each question or incomplete statement is followed by several suggested answers or completions. Select the one that BEST answers the question or completes the statement. *PRINT THE LETTER OF THE CORRECT ANSWER IN THE SPACE AT THE RIGHT.*

1. When conducting a needs assessment for the purpose of education planning, an agency's FIRST step is to identify or provide
    A. a profile of population characteristics
    B. barriers to participation
    C. existing resources
    D. profiles of competing resources

    1.____

2. Research has demonstrated that of the following, the MOST effective medium for communicating with external publics is(are)
    A. video news releases   B. television
    C. radio   D. newspapers

    2.____

3. Basic ideas behind the effort to influence the attitudes and behaviors of a constituency include each of the following EXCEPT the idea that
    A. words, rather than actions or events, are most likely to motivate
    B. demands for action are a usual response
    C. self-interest usually figures heavily into public involvement
    D. the reliability of change programs is difficult to assess

    3.____

4. An agency representative is trying to craft a pithy message to constituents in order to encourage the use of agency program resources.
   Choosing an audience for such messages is easiest when the message
    A. is project- or behavior-based   B. is combined with other messages
    C. is abstract   D. has a broad appeal

    4.____

5. Of the following factors, the MOST important to the success of an agency's external education or communication programs is the
    A. amount of resources used to implement them
    B. public's prior experiences with the agency
    C. real value of the program to the public
    D. commitment of the internal audience

    5.____

6. A representative for a state agency is being interviewed by a reporter from a local news network. The representative is being asked to defend a program that is extremely unpopular in certain parts of the municipality.
   When a constituency is known to be opposed to a position, the MOST useful communication strategy is to present

    6.____

93

A. only the arguments that are consistent with constituents' views
B. only the agency's side of the issue
C. both sides of the argument as clearly as possible
D. both sides of the argument, omitting key information about the opposing position

7. The MOST significant barriers to effective agency community relations include
   I. widespread distrust of communication strategies
   II. the media's "watchdog" stance
   III. public apathy
   IV. statutory opposition

   The CORRECT answer is:
   A. I only   B. I and II   C. II and III   D. III and IV

8. In conducting an education program, many agencies use workshops and seminars in a classroom setting.
   Advantages of classroom-style teaching over other means of educating the public include each of the following, EXCEPT
   A. enabling an instructor to verify learning through testing and interaction with the target audience
   B. enabling hands-on practice and other participatory learning techniques
   C. ability to reach an unlimited number of participants in a given length of time
   D. ability to convey the latest, most up-to-date information

9. The _____ model of community relations is characterized by an attempt to persuade the public to adopt the agency's point of view.
   A. two-way symmetric   B. two-way asymmetric
   C. public information   D. press agency/publicity

10. Important elements of an internal situation analysis include the
    I. list of agency opponents   II. communication audit
    III. updated organizational almanac   IV. stakeholder analysis

    The CORRECT answer is:
    A. I and II   B. I, II, and III   C. II and III   D. I, II, III and IV

11. Government agency information efforts typically involve each of the following objectives, EXCEPT to
    A. implement changes in the policies of government agencies to align with public opinion
    B. communicate the work of agencies
    C. explain agency techniques in a way that invites input from citizens
    D. provide citizen feedback to government administrators

12. Factors that are likely to influence the effectiveness of an educational campaign include the
    I. level of homogeneity among intended participants
    II. number and types of media used
    III. receptivity of the intended participants
    IV. level of specificity in the message or behavior to be taught

    The CORRECT answer is:
    A. I and II   B. I, II, and III   C. II and III   D. I, II, III, and IV

13. An agency representative is writing instructional objectives that will later help to measure the effectiveness of an educational program.
    Which of the following verbs, included in an objective, would be MOST helpful for the purpose of measuring effectiveness?
    A. Know   B. Identify   C. Learn   D. Comprehend

14. A state education agency wants to encourage participation in a program that has just received a boost through new federal legislation. The program is intended to include participants from a wide variety of socioeconomic and other demographic characteristics. The agency wants to launch a broad-based program that will inform virtually every interested party in the state about the program's new circumstances.
    In attempting to deliver this message to such a wide-ranging constituency, the agency's BEST practice would be to
    A. broadcast the same message through as many different media channels as possible
    B. focus on one discrete segment of the public at a time
    C. craft a message whose appeal is as broad as the public itself
    D. let the program's achievements speak for themselves and rely on word-of-mouth

15. Advantages associated with using the World Wide Web as an educational tool include
    I. an appeal to younger generations of the public
    II. visually-oriented, interactive learning
    III. learning that is not confined by space, time, or institutional association
    IV. a variety of methods for verifying use and learning

    The CORRECT answer is:
    A. I only   B. I and II   C. I, II, and III   D. I, II, II, and IV

16. In agencies involved in health care, community relations is a critical function because it
    A. serves as an intermediary between the agency and consumers
    B. generates a clear mission statement for agency goals and priorities
    C. ensures patient privacy while satisfying the media's right to information
    D. helps marketing professionals determine the wants and needs of agency constituents

17. After an extensive campaign to promote its newest program to constituents, an agency learns that most of the audience did not understand the intended message.
MOST likely, the agency has
   A. chosen words that were intended to inform, rather than persuade
   B. not accurately interpreted what the audience really needed to know
   C. overestimated the ability of the audience to receive and process the message
   D. compensated for noise that may have interrupted the message

18. The necessary elements that lead to conviction and motivation in the minds of participants in an educational or information program include each of the following, EXCEPT the _____ of the message.
   A. acceptability   B. intensity
   C. single-channel appeal   D. pervasiveness

19. Printed materials are often at the core of educational programs provided by public agencies.
The PRIMARY disadvantage associated with print is that it
   A. does not enable comprehensive treatment of a topic
   B. is generally unreliable in term of assessing results
   C. is often the most expensive medium available
   D. is constrained by time

20. Traditional thinking on public opinion holds that there is about _____ percent of the public who are pivotal to shifting the balance and momentum of opinion—they are concerned about an issue, but not fanatical, and interested enough to pay attention to a reasoned discussion.
   A. 2   B. 10   C. 33   D. 51

21. One of the most useful guidelines for influencing attitude change among people is to
   A. invite the target audience to come to you, rather than approaching them
   B. use moral appeals as the primary approach
   C. use concrete images to enable people to see the results of behaviors or indifference
   D. offer tangible rewards to people for changes in behavior

22. An agency is attempting to evaluate the effectiveness of its educational program. For this purpose, it wants to observe several focus groups discussing the same program.
Which of the following would NOT be a guideline for the use of focus groups?
   A. Focus groups should only include those who have participated in the program.
   B. Be sure to accurately record the discussion.
   C. The same questions should be asked at each focus group meeting.
   D. It is often helpful to have a neutral, non-agency employee facilitate discussions.

5 (#1)

23. Research consistently shows that _____ is the determinant most likely to make a newspaper editor run a news release.
    A. novelty   B. prominence   C. proximity   D. conflict

24. Which of the following is NOT one of the major variables to take into account when considering a population-needs assessment?
    A. State of program development   B. Resources available
    C. Demographics   D. Community attitudes

25. The FIRST step in any communications audit is to
    A. develop a research instrument
    B. determine how the organization currently communicates
    C. hire a contractor
    D. determine which audience to assess

KEY (CORRECT ANSWERS)

1.	A		11.	A
2.	D		12.	D
3.	A		13.	B
4.	A		14.	B
5.	D		15.	C
6.	C		16.	A
7.	D		17.	B
8.	C		18.	C
9.	B		19.	B
10.	C		20.	B

21. C
22. A
23. C
24. C
25. D

TEST 2

DIRECTIONS: Each question or incomplete statement is followed by several suggested answers or completions. Select the one that BEST answers the question or completes the statement. *PRINT THE LETTER OF THE CORRECT ANSWER IN THE SPACE AT THE RIGHT.*

1. A public relations practitioner at an agency has just composed a press release highlighting a program's recent accomplishments and success stories.
   In pitching such releases to print outlets, the practitioner should
   I. e-mail, mail, or send them by messenger
   II. address them to "editor" or "news director"
   III. have an assistant call all media contacts by telephone
   IV. ask reporters or editors how they prefer to receive them

   The CORRECT answer is:
   A. I and II   B. I and IV   C. II, III, and IV   D. III only

2. The "output goals" of an educational program are MOST likely to include
   A. specified ratings of services by participants on a standardized scale
   B. observable effects on a given community or clientele
   C. the number of instructional hours provided
   D. the number of participants served

3. An agency wants to evaluate satisfaction levels among program participants, and mails out questionnaires to everyone who has been enrolled in the last year.
   The PRIMARY problem associated with this method of evaluative research is that it
   A. poses a significant inconvenience for respondents
   B. is inordinately expensive
   C. does not allow for follow-up or clarification questions
   D. usually involves a low response rate

4. A communications audit is an important tool for measuring
   A. the depth of penetration of a particular message or program
   B. the cost of the organization's information campaigns
   C. how key audiences perceive an organization
   D. the commitment of internal stakeholders

5. The "ABCs" of written learning objectives include each of the following, EXCEPT
   A. Audience   B. Behavior   C. Conditions   D. Delineation

6. When attempting to change the behaviors of constituents, it is important to keep in mind that
   I. most people are skeptical of communications that try to get them to change their behaviors
   II. in most cases, a person selects the media to which he exposes himself
   III. people tend to react defensively to messages or programs that rely on fear as a motivating factor
   IV. programs should aim for the broadest appeal possible in order to include as many participants as possible

   The CORRECT answer is:
   A. I and II   B. I, II and III   C. II and III   D. I, II, III, and IV

7. The "laws" of public opinion include the idea that it is
   A. useful for anticipating emergencies
   B. not sensitive to important events
   C. basically determined by self-interest
   D. sustainable through persistent appeals

8. Which of the following types of evaluations is used to measure public attitudes before and after an information/educational program?
   A. Retrieval study
   B. Copy test
   C. Quota sampling
   D. Benchmark study

9. The PRIMARY source for internal communications is(are) usually
   A. flow charts
   B. meetings
   C. voice mail
   D. printed publications

10. An agency representative is putting together informational materials—brochures and a newsletter—outlining changes in one of the state's biggest benefits programs.
    In assembling print materials as a medium for delivering information to the public, the representative should keep in mind each of the following trends:
    I. For various reasons, the reading capabilities of the public are in general decline
    II. Without tables and graphs to help illustrate the changes, it is unlikely that the message will be delivered effectively
    III. Professionals and career-oriented people are highly receptive to information written in the form of a journal article or empirical study
    IV. People tend to be put off by print materials that use itemized and bulleted (●) lists

    The CORRECT answer is:
    A. I and II   B. I, II and III   C. II and III   D. I, II, III, and IV

11. Which of the following steps in a problem-oriented information campaign would typically be implemented FIRST?
    A. Deciding on tactics
    B. Determining a communications strategy
    C. Evaluating the problem's impact
    D. Developing an organizational strategy

12. A common pitfall in conducting an educational program is to
    A. aim it at the wrong target audience
    B. overfund it
    C. leave it in the hands of people who are in the business of education, rather than those with expertise in the business of the organization
    D. ignore the possibility that some other organization is meeting the same educational need for the target audience

13. The key factors that affect the credibility of an agency's educational program include
    A. organization
    B. scope
    C. sophistication
    D. penetration

14. Research on public opinion consistently demonstrates that it is
    A. easy to move people toward a strong opinion on anything, as long as they are approached directly through their emotions
    B. easier to move people away from an opinion they currently hold than to have them form an opinion about something they have not previously cared about
    C. easy to move people toward a strong opinion on anything, as long as the message appeals to their reason and intellect
    D. difficult to move people toward a strong opinion on anything, no matter what the approach

15. In conducting an education program, many agencies use meetings and conferences to educate an audience about the organization and its programs. Advantages associated with this approach include
    I. a captive audience that is known to be interested in the topic
    II. ample opportunities for verifying learning
    III. cost-efficient meeting space
    IV. the ability to provide information on a wider variety of subjects

    The CORRECT answer is:
    A. I and II   B. I, III and IV   C. II and III   D. I, II, III and IV

16. An agency is attempting to evaluate the effectiveness of its educational programs. For this purpose, it wants to observe several focus groups discussing particular programs.
    For this purpose, a focus group should never number more than _____ participants.
    A. 5   B. 10   C. 15   D. 20

17. A _____ speech is written so that several agency members can deliver it to different audiences with only minor variations.
    A. basic   B. printed   C. quota   D. pattern

18. Which of the following statements about public opinion is generally considered to be FALSE?
    A. Opinion is primarily reactive rather than proactive.
    B. People have more opinions about goals than about the means by which to achieve them.
    C. Facts tend to shift opinion in the accepted direction when opinion is not solidly structured.
    D. Public opinion is based more on information than desire.

19. An agency is trying to promote its educational program.
    As a general rule, the agency should NOT assume that
    A. people will only participate if they perceive an individual benefit
    B. promotions need to be aimed at small, discrete groups
    C. if the program is good, the audience will find out about it
    D. a variety of methods, including advertising, special events, and direct mail, should be considered

20. In planning a successful educational program, probably the first and most important question for an agency to ask is:
    A. What will be the content of the program?
    B. Who will be served by the program?
    C. When is the best time to schedule the program?
    D. Why is the program necessary?

21. Media kits are LEAST likely to contain
    A. fact sheets   B. memoranda
    C. photographs with captions D. news releases

22. The use of pamphlets and booklets as media for communication with the public often involves the disadvantage that
    A. the messages contained within them are frequently nonspecific
    B. it is difficult to measure their effectiveness in delivering the message
    C. there are few opportunities for people to refer to them
    D. color reproduction is poor

23. The MOST important prerequisite of a good educational program is an
    A. abundance of resources to implement it
    B. individual staff unit formed for the purpose of program delivery
    C. accurate needs assessment
    D. uneducated constituency

24. After an education program has been delivered, an agency conducts a program evaluation to determine whether its objectives have been met.
General rules about how to conduct such an education program valuation include each of the following, EXCEPT that it
   A. must be done immediately after the program has been implemented
   B. should be simple and easy to use
   C. should be designed so that tabulation of responses can take place quickly and inexpensively
   D. should solicit mostly subjective, open-ended responses if the audience was large

25. Using electronic media such as television as means of educating the public is typically recommended ONLY for agencies that
   I. have a fairly simple message to begin with
   II. want to reach the masses, rather than a targeted audience
   III. have substantial financial resources
   IV. accept that they will not be able to measure the results of the campaign with much precision

   The CORRECT answer is:
   A. I and II   B. I, II and III   C. II and IV   D. I, II, III and IV

KEY (CORRECT ANSWERS)

1.	B	11.	C
2.	C	12.	D
3.	D	13.	A
4.	C	14.	D
5.	D	15.	B
6.	B	16.	B
7.	C	17.	D
8.	D	18.	D
9.	D	19.	C
10.	A	20.	D

21.	B
22.	B
23.	C
24.	D
25.	D

PREPARING WRITTEN MATERIALS
EXAMINATION SECTION
TEST 1

DIRECTIONS: Each question contains a sentence. Read each sentence carefully to decide whether it is correct. Then, in the space at the right, mark your answer:
- A. If the sentence is incorrect because of bad grammar or sentence structure;
- B. If the sentence is incorrect because of bad punctuation
- C. If the sentence is incorrect because of bad capitalization
- D. If the sentence is correct.

Each incorrect sentence has only one type of error. Consider a sentence correct if it has no errors, although there may be other correct ways of saying the same thing.

SAMPLE QUESTION i: One of our clerks were promoted yesterday.

The subject of this sentence is *one*, so the verb should be *was promoted* instead of *were promoted*. Since the sentence is incorrect because of bad grammar, the answer to Sample Question I is A.

SAMPLE QUESTION II: Between you and me, I would prefer not going there.

Since this sentence is correct, the answer to Sample Question II is D.

1. The National alliance of Businessmen is trying to persuade private businesses to hire youth in the summertime.　　1.____

2. The supervisor who is on vacation, is in charge of processing vouchers.　　2.____

3. The activity of the committee at its conferences is always stimulating.　　3.____

4. After checking the addresses again, the letters went to the mailroom.　　4.____

5. The director, as well as the employees, are interested in sharing the dividends.　　5.____

6. The experiments conducted by professor Alford were described at a recent meeting of our organization.　　6.____

7. I shall be glad to discuss these matters with whoever represents the Municipal Credit Union.　　7.____

8. In my opinion, neither Mr. Price nor Mr. Roth knows how to operate this office appliance.　　8.____

9. The supervisor, as well as the other stenographers, were unable to transcribe Miss Johnson's shorthand notes. 9._____

10. Important functions such as, recruiting and training, are performed by our unit. 10._____

11. Realizing that many students are interested in this position, we sent announcements to all the High Schools. 11._____

12. After pointing out certain incorrect conclusions, the report was revised by Mr. Clark and submitted to Mr. Batson. 12._____

13. The employer contributed two hundred dollars; the employees, one hundred dollars. 13._____

14. He realized that the time, when a supervisor could hire and fire, was over. 14._____

15. The complaints received by Commissioner Regan was the cause of the change in policy. 15._____

16. Any report, that is to be sent to the Federal Security Administration, must be approved and signed by Mr. Yound. 16._____

17. Of the two stenographers, Miss Rand is the more accurate. 17._____

18. Since the golf courses are crowded during the summer, more men are needed to maintain the courses in good playing condition. 18._____

19. Although he invited Mr. Frankel and I to attend a meeting of the Civil Service Assembly, we were unable to accept his invitation. 19._____

20. Only the employees who worked overtime last week may leave one hour earlier today. 20._____

21. We need someone who can speak french fluently. 21._____

22. A tall, elderly, man entered the office and asked to see Mr. Brown. 22._____

23. The clerk insisted that he had filed the correspondence in the proper cabinet. 23._____

24. "Will you assist us," he asked? 24._____

25. According to the information contained in the report, a large quantity of paper and envelopes were used by this bureau last year. 25._____

KEY (CORRECT ANSWERS)

1.	C	11.	C
2.	B	12.	A
3.	D	13.	D
4.	A	14.	B
5.	A	15.	A
6.	C	16.	B
7.	D	17.	D
8.	D	18.	C
9.	A	19.	A
10.	B	20.	D

21.	C
22.	B
23.	D
24.	B
25.	A

TEST 2

DIRECTIONS: Each question consists of a sentence which may be classified appropriately under one of the following four categories:
- A. Incorrect because of faulty grammar or sentence structure.
- B. Incorrect because of faulty punctuation.
- C. Incorrect because of faulty capitalization.
- D. Correct

Examine each sentence carefully. Then, in the space at the right, print the capital letter preceding the option which is the BEST of the four suggested above. All incorrect sentences contain only one type of error. Consider a sentence correct if it contains none of the types of errors mentioned, although there may be other correct ways of expressing the same thought.

1. Mrs. Black the supervisor of the unit, has many important duties. 1._____
2. We spoke to the man whom you saw yesterday. 2._____
3. When a holiday falls on sunday, it is officially celebrated on monday. 3._____
4. Of the two reports submitted, this one is the best. 4._____
5. Each staff member, including the accountants, were invited to the meeting. 5._____
6. Give the package to whomever calls for it. 6._____
7. To plan the work is our responsibility; to carry it out is his. 7._____
8. "May I see the person in charge of this office," asked the visitor? 8._____
9. He knows that it was not us who prepared the report. 9._____
10. These problems were brought to the attention of senator Johnson. 10._____
11. The librarian classifies all books periodicals and documents. 11._____
12. Any employee who uses an adding machine realizes its importance. 12._____
13. Instead of coming to the office, the clerk should of come to the supply room. 13._____
14. He asked, "will your staff assist us?" 14._____
15. Having been posted on the bulletin board, we were certain that the announcements would be read. 15._____
16. He was not informed, that he would have to work overtime. 16._____
17. The wind blew several paper off of his desk. 17._____

18. Charles Dole, who is a member of the committee, was asked to confer with commissioner Wilson. 18.____

19. Miss Bell will issue a copy to whomever asks for one. 19.____

20. Most employees, and he is no exception do not like to work overtime. 20.____

21. This is the man whom you interviewed last week. 21.____

22. Of the two cities visited, White Plains is the cleanest. 22.____

23. Although he was willing to work on other holidays, he refused to work on Labor day. 23.____

24. If an employee wishes to attend the conference, he should fill out the necessary forms. 24.____

25. The division chief reports that an engineer and an inspector is needed for this special survey. 25.____

KEY (CORRECT ANSWERS)

1.	B		11.	B
2.	D		12.	D
3.	C		13.	A
4.	A		14.	C
5.	A		15.	A
6.	A		16.	B
7.	D		17.	A
8.	B		18.	C
9.	A		19.	A
10.	C		20.	B

21. D
22. A
23. C
24. D
25. A

TEST 3

DIRECTIONS: Each question consists of a sentence which may be classified appropriately under one of the following four categories:
- A. Incorrect because of faulty grammar or sentence structure.
- B. Incorrect because of faulty punctuation.
- C. Incorrect because of faulty capitalization.
- D. Correct

Examine each sentence carefully. Then, in the space at the right, print the capital letter preceding the option which is the BEST of the four suggested above. All incorrect sentences contain only one type of error. Consider a sentence correct if it contains none of the types of errors mentioned, although there may be other correct ways of expressing the same thought.

1. We have learned that there was more than twelve people present at the meeting. 1.____

2. Every one of the employees is able to do this kind of work. 2.____

3. Neither the supervisor nor his assistant are in the office today. 3.____

4. The office manager announced that any clerk, who volunteered for the assignment, would be rewarded. 4.____

5. After looking carefully in all the files, the letter was finally found on a desk. 5.____

6. In answer to the clerk's question, the supervisor said, "this assignment must be completed today." 6.____

7. The office manager says that he can permit only you and me to go to the meeting. 7.____

8. The supervisor refused to state who he would assign to the reception unit. 8.____

9. At the last meeting, he said that he would interview us in september. 9.____

10. Mr. Jones, who is one of our most experienced employees has been placed in charge of the main office. 10.____

11. I think that this adding machine is the most useful of the two we have in our office. 11.____

12. Between you and I, our new stenographer is not as competent as our former stenographer. 12.____

13. The new assignment should be given to whoever can do the work rapidly 13.____

14. Mrs. Smith, as well as three other typists, was assigned to the new office. 14.____

2 (#3)

15. The staff assembled for the conference on time but, the main speaker arrived late. 15.____

16. The work was assigned to Miss Green and me. 16.____

17. The staff regulations state that an employee, who is frequently tardy, may receive a negative evaluation. 17.____

18. He is the kind of person who is always willing to undertake difficult assignments. 18.____

19. Mr. Wright's request cannot be granted under no conditions. 19.____

20. George Colt a new employee, was asked to deliver the report to the Domestic Relations Court. 20.____

21. The supervisor entered the room and said, "The work must be completed today." 21.____

22. The employees were given their assignments and, they were asked to begin work immediately. 22.____

23. The letter will be sent to the United States senate this week. 23.____

24. When the supervisor entered the room, he noticed that the book was laying on the desk. 24.____

25. The price of the pens were higher than the price of the pencils. 25.____

KEY (CORRECT ANSWERS)

1.	A	11.	A
2.	D	12.	A
3.	A	13.	D
4.	B	14.	D
5.	A	15.	B
6.	C	16.	D
7.	D	17.	B
8.	A	18.	D
9.	C	19.	A
10.	B	20.	B

21. D
22. B
23. C
24. A
25. A

PREPARING WRITTEN MATERIAL

PARAGRAPH REARRANGEMENT
COMMENTARY

The sentences that follow are in scrambled order. You are to rearrange them in proper order and indicate the letter choice containing the correct answer at the space at the right.

Each group of sentences in this section is actually a paragraph presented in scrambled order. Each sentence in the group has a place in that paragraph; no sentence is to be left out. You are to read each group of sentences and decide upon the best order in which to put the sentences so as to form a well-organized paragraph.

The questions in this section measure the ability to solve a problem when all the facts relevant to its solution are not given.

More specifically, certain positions of responsibility and authority require the employee to discover connection between events sometimes, apparently, unrelated. In order to do this, the employee will find it necessary to correctly infer that unspecified events have probably occurred or are likely to occur. This ability becomes especially important when action must be taken on incomplete information.

Accordingly, these questions require competitors to choose among several suggested alternatives, each of which presents a different sequential arrangement of the events. Competitors must choose the MOST logical of the suggested sequences.

In order to do so, they may be required to draw on general knowledge to infer missing concepts or events that are essential to sequencing the given events. Competitors should be careful to infer only what is essential to the sequence. The plausibility of the wrong alternatives will always require the inclusion of unlikely events or of additional chains of events which are NOT essential to sequencing the given events.

It's very important to remember that you are looking for the best of the four possible choices, and that the best choice of all may not even be one of the answers you're given to choose from.

There is no one right way to solve these problems. Many people have found it helpful to first write out the order of the sentences, as they would have arranged them, on their scrap paper before looking at the possible answers. If their optimum answer is there, this can save them some time. If it isn't, this method can still give insight into solving the problem. Others find it most helpful to just go through each of the possible choices, contrasting each as they go along. You should use whatever method feels comfortable and works for you.

While most of these types of questions are not that difficult, we've added a higher percentage of the difficult type, just to give you more practice. Usually there are only one or two questions on this section that contain such subtle distinctions that you're unable to answer confidently. And you then may find yourself stuck deciding between two possible choices, neither of which you're sure about.

EXAMINATION SECTION
TEST 1

DIRECTIONS: Each group of sentences in this section is actually a paragraph presented in scrambled order. Each sentence in the group has a place in that paragraph; no sentence is to be left out. You are to read each group of sentences, so as to form a well-organized paragraph. Before trying to answer the questions which follow each group of sentences, jot down the correct order of the sentences. Then answer each of the questions by printing the letter of the correct answer in the space at the right. Remember that you will receive credit only for answers marked.

    P. The infant only feels the positive stimulation of warmth and food and does not differentiate the warmth and food from their source, mother.
    Q. The infant, at the moment of birth, would feel the fear of dying if gracious fate did not preserve it from any awareness of the anxiety involved in the separation from mother.
    R. The infant's state, then, is what has been called narcissism.
    S. Mother is warmth, mother is food, mother is the euphoric state of satisfaction and security.
    T. Even after being born, the infant is not yet aware of itself, and of the world as being outside of itself.

1. Which sentence did you put before Sentence Q?   1._____

    A. P
    B. R
    C. S
    D. T
    E. None of the above. Sentence Q is first.

2. Which sentence did you put after Sentence S?   2._____

    A. P
    B. Q
    C. R
    D. T
    E. None of the above. Sentence S is last.

3. Which sentence did you put before Sentence P?   3._____

    A. Q
    B. R
    C. S
    D. T
    E. None of the above. Sentence P is first.

4. Which sentence did you put after Sentence P?

    A. Q
    B. R
    C. S
    D. T
    E. None of the above. Sentence P is last.

5. Which sentence did you put after Sentence R?

    A. P
    B. Q
    C. S
    D. T
    E. None of the above. Sentence R is last.

KEY (CORRECT ANSWERS)

1. E
2. C
3. D
4. C
5. E

TEST 2

1. C
2. E
3. B
4. A
5. A

2 (#2)

KEY (CORRECT ANSWERS)

1. A
2. E
3. B
4. D
5. C

———

TEST 3

DIRECTIONS: Each group of sentences in this section is actually a paragraph presented in scrambled order. Each sentence in the group has a place in that paragraph; no sentence is to be left out. You are to read each group of sentences, so as to form a well-organized paragraph. Before trying to answer the questions which follow each group of sentences, jot down the correct order of the sentences. Then answer each of the questions by printing the letter of the correct answer in the space at the right. Remember that you will receive credit only for answers marked.

P. Indeed, in his time, Freud's theories of sex had a challenging and revolutionary character.
Q. Sexual mores have changed so much that Freud's theories no longer are shocking to the middle classes.
R. Freud has been criticized for his overevaluation of sex.
S. But what was true sixty years ago is no longer true.
T. This criticism resulted from a wish to remove an element from Freud's system which might arouse criticism among conventionally-minded people.

1. Which sentence did you put last?
   A. P B. Q C. R D. S E. T

2. Which sentence did you put before Sentence Q?
   A. P
   B. R
   C. S
   D. T
   E. None of the above. Sentence Q is first.

3. Which sentence did you put after Sentence T?
   A. P
   B. Q
   C. R
   D. S
   E. None of the above. Sentence T is last.

4. Which sentence did you put before Sentence R?
   A. P
   B. Q
   C. S
   D. T
   E. None of the above. Sentence R is first.

5. Which sentence did you put after Sentence R?
   A. P
   B. Q
   C. S
   D. T
   E. None of the above. Sentence R is last.

KEY (CORRECT ANSWERS)

1. B
2. C
3. A
4. E
5. D

TEST 4

DIRECTIONS: Each group of sentences in this section is actually a paragraph presented in scrambled order. Each sentence in the group has a place in that paragraph; no sentence is to be left out. You are to read each group of sentences, so as to form a well-organized paragraph. Before trying to answer the questions which follow each group of sentences, jot down the correct order of the sentences. Then answer each of the questions by printing the letter of the correct answer in the space at the right. Remember that you will receive credit only for answers marked.

P. Early Scandanavian accounts, as well, are too mythological and legendary to serve as history.
Q. The first trustworthy written evidence of a kingdom of Denmark belongs to the beginning of the Viking period.
R. Ancient Roman knowledge of this remote country was fragmentary and unreliable.
S. Archaeology and the study of place names, however, provide a certain amount of information about the earliest settlements.
T. Everything before that is prehistory.

1. Which sentence did you put fourth?
   A. P   B. B. Q   C. C. R   D. D. S   E. E. T

2. Which sentence did you put after Sentence T?
   A. Q
   B. R
   C. S
   D. None of the above. Sentence T is last.

3. Which sentence did you put after Sentence Q?
   A. P
   B. R
   C. S
   D. T
   E. None of the above. Sentence Q is last.

4. Which sentence did you put before Sentence Q?
   A. P
   B. R
   C. S
   D. T
   E. None of the above. Sentence Q is first.

5. Which sentence did you put after Sentence P?
   A. Q
   B. R
   C. S
   D. T
   E. None of the above. Sentence P is last.

KEY (CORRECT ANSWERS)

1. A
2. C
3. D
4. E
5. C

———

TEST 5

DIRECTIONS: Each group of sentences in this section is actually a paragraph presented in scrambled order. Each sentence in the group has a place in that paragraph; no sentence is to be left out. You are to read each group of sentences, so as to form a well-organized paragraph. Before trying to answer the questions which follow each group of sentences, jot down the correct order of the sentences. Then answer each of the questions by printing the letter of the correct answer in the space at the right. Remember that you will receive credit only for answers marked.

P. In 1268, ambassadors were required to surrender all gifts they had received on their missions.
Q. In the 13th century, the Venetian republic began to lay down rules of conduct for its ambassadors.
R. In 1288, it was decreed that ambassadors were to report in writing on the results of their missions.
S. Such reports are a mine of historical material.
T. It is in Venice that the origins of modern diplomacy are to be sought.

1. Which sentence did you put second?
   A. P   B. Q   C. R   D. S   E. T

2. Which sentence did you put after Sentence R?
   A. P
   B. Q
   C. S
   D. T
   E. None of the above. Sentence R is last.

3. Which sentence did you put before Sentence P?
   A. Q
   B. R
   C. S
   D. T
   E. None of the above. Sentence P is first.

4. Which sentence did you put before Sentence T?
   A. P
   B. Q
   C. R
   D. S
   E. None of the above. Sentence T is first.

5. Which sentence did you put last?
   A. P   B. B. Q   C. C. R   D. D. S   E. E. T

KEY (CORRECT ANSWERS)

1. B
2. C
3. A
4. E
5. D

BASIC FUNDAMENTALS OF VITAMINS

I. WHAT ARE VITAMINS?

They are a group of organic (carbon-containing) compounds that regulate reactions occurring in metabolism—the process by which the body breaks down and uses foods. Once called accessory food factors, vitamins are necessary because, just as water needs heat to boil, certain processes in the body won't occur properly without vitamins. Scientists don't fully understand why. The most popular theory is that the vitamins serve as traffic controllers, telling the body when certain procedures may begin, or determining speed and duration. Thus, the absence of a vitamin may block a reaction in a cell, thereby disrupting the cell's balance and causing it to form improperly or function abnormally.

Unlike some other organisms, the human body does not manufacture vitamins, and needs to acquire them from diet. Scientists now think that the reason is built in, a result of evolution. In the beginning, the theory goes, simple organisms could get everything they needed straight from the environment. But as life forms became more complex, the ability to make those compounds directly from elements in nature was lost. And in the case of vitamin C, they think that our body's inability to synthesize it is a form of *genetic disease*. That is, we did not discard the ability on the way to becoming *man*, but rather something went wrong in the formation of our metabolic process so that the ingredients we need to make vitamin C are completely missing.

Vitamins are subdivided into two basic classifications—water-soluble and fat-soluble.

Water-soluble vitamins (except vitamin C) serve as catalysts in metabolic activity. They help the body transfer energy from food, and aid in breaking down fats, carbohydrates, and proteins. During digestion, those vitamins are absorbed into the intestine - where no chemical reaction is needed to make them usable - and then pass directly to the bloodstream, where they are carried to body tissues for use. Each of the water-soluble vitamins serves a very special function in the body. For example, vitamins B_1 and B_6 control the conversion of carbohydrates and proteins into metabolic energy (calories), while niacin and riboflavin transport hydrogen during metabolism, thereby causing specific proteins, fats, and carbohydrates to be formed. Vitamin C aids in the formation of collagen, the connective tissue of skin, tendons, and bone, and in absorption and use of iron and potassium. Water-soluble vitamins are not normally stored in the body.

The fat-soluble vitamins are a much more sophisticated group. They serve more highly specialized functions and are much more selectively distributed in nature. They include vitamins A, D, E, and K, all of which can be stored in the body and can be toxic when taken in excess. The fat-solubles are necessary for the synthesis of some body enzymes (substances that speed up or start chemical reactions in the body), and form part of many biological membranes. They are transported by lymph from the intestines to the circulating blood. More fat-solubles than water-solubles are stored in the body, with A, D, and K stored in the liver and vitamin E stored in body fat. Also, since fat is necessary to break down those vitamins, anything that impedes fat metabolism can inhibit their use.

One of the best ways to make sure that your diet is providing your body with what it needs is to make sure that it is varied. It doesn't really matter if you do not savor a few members of any of the basic food groups, since there are enough other foods rich in the same nutrients to take up the slack. You don't have to eat liver to get iron, if you dislike it. Eat spinach in a salad instead and get plenty of iron and some vitamin A too.

Contrary to the faddist notion, the idea of taking each little vitamin in a separate tablet (as opposed to the more common multiple-vitamin tablet) is wrong. What people are doing by this practice is spending a good deal of money and taking the chance of vitamin overdose. It is simply useless to load the body with substances it can't possibly utilize.

In fact, the whole idea of vitamin pills is superfluous unless a person (1) has an illness that eliminates an entire food group from the diet, (2) is the sort of vegetarian who eschews eggs, butter, milk, cheese, and all meats, poultry, and fish, or (3) is pregnant, sick or so poor that a varied, quality diet is impossible. If you are in doubt about your supply of vitamins, ask your physician for advice and take only those prescribed.

Also, people should interpret in a common-sense way the *recommended daily requirement* phrase. This simply refers to an optimum amount that scientists have found to be healthy for humans. One will find that the United States requires one amount, Canada another, and some other country another. This doesn't at all mean that, if you're getting less than this amount of a vitamin, you're deficient.

II. FAT-SOLUBLE VITAMINS

Vitamin	Uses	Possible Results of Deficiency	Possible Results of Surplus	Sources
A (Retinol)	Serves in the formation of normal skin and the mucosa, internal skin, bone, and tooth formation, night and color vision	Deterioration of skin, faulty bone and tooth development, deterioration of eyes, night blindness and blindness	Drying and peeling of skin, loss of hair, bone, and joint pain, fragile bones, enlarged liver and spleen; in severe cases, death	Liver, butter, and fortified margarine, cream, whole milk and cheese made from whole milk, carrots, and dark green leafy vegetables
D	Regulates intestinal absorption of calcium and phosphorus and utilization of those minerals in bones and soft tissue, and plays a part in protein metabolism	In children: delayed tooth development, large joints, soft bones that are easily deformed and broken, deformities of chest, skull, spine, and pelvis (rickets). In adults: osteo-malacia (adult rickets), characterized by softening of bones	Weakness, weight loss, vomiting, diarrhea, calcium deposits in soft tissues, kidney damage and death	Formed by direct exposure of skin to sunlight, fortified milk, fish liver oils; also, small amounts of butter made in the summer, liver, egg yolk, and fatty fish like sardines, salmon, and tuna

Vitamin	Uses	Possible Results of Deficiency	Possible Results of Surplus	Sources
E	An antioxidant to reduce oxidation of vitamin A, the carotenes, and polyunsaturated fatty acids	Deficiency (rare and even difficult to produce experimentally) causes mild anemia and destruction of red blood cells	Excess (although there is no conclusive evidence) is believed to cause muscle damage and fatigue	Vegetable oils like cottonseed, safflower, sunflower, soybean; corn, almonds, peanuts, wheat germ, rice germ, asparagus, green leafy vegetables, liver, margarine, vegetable shortening
K	Necessary for proper clotting of blood	Leads to prolonged clotting time and hemorrhagic disease in newborn infants	Excess of menaquinone, a synthetic form, can cause jaundice in newborn infants, but natural forms have not been found to be toxic. An excess in adults is unlikely.	The main source is synthesis by normal bacteria in the intestine, a function that can be inhibited by some antibiotics. Food sources include lettuce, spinach, kale, cauliflower, cabbage, liver, egg yolk, soybean oils.

III. WATER-SOLUBLE VITAMINS

Vitamin	Uses	Possible Results of Deficiency	Possible Results of Surplus	Sources
C (Ascorbic Acid)	Aids in the formation of collagen, the connective tissue of skin, tendons, and bone, in the formation of hemoglobin, the absorption and use of iron and phosphorus, and possibly in the metabolism of protein and carbohydrates.	Poor bone and tooth development, bleeding gums, weakened cartilage and capillary walls, skin hemorrhages, anemia (scurvy)	A possible factor in the destruction of vitamin B_{12} in ingested food.	Citrus fruits, tomatoes, cantaloupe, and other melons, berries, green leafy vegetables, peppers, broccoli, cauliflower, and fresh potatoes

Vitamin	Uses	Possible Results of Deficiency	Possible Results of Surplus	Sources
B_1 (Thiamine)	Necessary for carbohydrate metabolism	Apathy, depression, poor appetite, lack of tone in the gastrointestinal tract, constipation, heart failure (beriberi)	No known effects	Whole-grain flours and cereals, wheat germ, seeds like sunflower and sesame, nuts like peanuts and pine nuts, legumes like soybeans, organ meats, pork (one of the richest sources) and leafy vegetables
B_2 (Riboflavin)	Used in enzymes that transport hydrogen in the body as part of the metabolism of carbohydrates, fats, and proteins	Cracks at corners of lips, scaly skin around nose and ears, sore tongue and mouth, itching, burning eyes, sensitivity to light	No known effects	Liver, kidney, cheese, milk, eggs, leafy vegetables, enriched bread, lean meat, beans, and peas
Niacin	Forms part of co-enzymes needed for hydrogen transport and for health of tissue cells	Skin rash, sore mouth and tongue, inflamed membranes in the digestive tract, depression, mental disorientation and stupor (pellagra)	Flushing of skin and occasionally jaundice	Organ meats, lean meats, poultry, fish, wheat germ and whole-grain flours and cereals, nuts, seeds, rice, beans, and peas. The amino acid tryptophan can be converted to niacin in the body
B_6	Used in metabolism of protein, essential for conversion of the amino acid tryptophan to niacin in the body	Dermatitis around eyes, at angles of mouth, sore mouth and smooth red tongue, weight loss, dizziness, vomiting, anemia, kidney stones, nervous disturbances and convulsions	No known effects	Seeds like sunflower, wheat germ and bran, whole-grain bread, flours and cereals, liver, meats, fish and poultry, potatoes, beans and brown rice

Vitamin	Uses	Possible Results of Deficiency	Possible Results of Surplus	Sources
Pantothenic acid	Essential to many chemical reactions, particularly metabolism and release of energy from fat, protein, and carbohydrates	Unlikely unless a part of total B vitamin deficiency. Unless the diet consists solely of highly processed foods, this deficiency is seldom seen	No known effects	Liver, eggs, wheat germ, peanuts, and peas; widely distributed in most foods
Biotin	Essential for metabolism of protein, fats, and carbohydrates and energy release	Dermatitis, loss of appetite, nausea, insomnia, deep depression, and muscle pain. Occurs only when large quantities of raw egg whites are consumed over a long period since audin, a protein in raw egg white, blocks absorption of biotin	No known effects	Widely distributed in food, but the best sources are liver, egg yolk, nuts, and legumes
Folic Acid	Essential for the synthesis of nucleic acids, the building blocks life	Smooth red tongue, intestinal distress, macrocytic of anemia and failure of young red blood cells to mature	No known effects	Liver, leafy vegetables, dried beans and peas, asparagus and broccoli, fresh oranges, whole wheat flours, breads, and cereals
B_{12}	Synthesis of nucleic acids and the amino acid, aspartic acid	Sore tongue, weakness, weight loss, tingling hands and feet, back pain, mental and nervous changes, eventually pernicious anemia, and irreversible deterioration of the spinal cord	No known effects	Only in animal foods like liver, meats, poultry, fish, and shellfish, eggs and milk and milk products

Glossary of Dietary Terms

CONTENTS

		Page
Absorption	Available	1
Avidin	Carbohydrate	2
Carob powder	Denaturation	3
Dixtrin	Exchange list	4
Excipient	Hyperkalemia	5
Hyperlipoproteinemia	Lactose intolerance	6
Lecithin	Mineral oil	7
Monosaccharides	Pasteurized	8
Pellagra	Saccharin	9
Salt	Urea	10
Uremia	Zinc	11

Glossary of Dietary Terms

Absorption. Assimilation or taking up of nutrients, fluids, gases, or other substances by the stomach or intestinal walls following digestion.

Acetone (dimethyl ketone). Product of incomplete oxidation of fats. May occur in diabetes mellitus, giving a fruity odor to the breath.

Acid-forming foods. Foods in which the acidic residue exceeds the alkaline residue.

Acidosis. An abnormal increase of acids in the blood caused by accumulation of an excess of acids in the body or by excessive loss of base; characterized by a fall in the pH of the blood or decrease in the alkali reserve in the body. Examples of acidosis include the ketosis (of diabetes mellitus), phosphoric, sulfuric, and hydrochloric acids (of renal insufficiency), lactic acid (or prolonged exercise), and carbonic acid (in respiratory disease).

ADA. Abbreviation for the American Dietetic Association, American Diabetes Association, and American Dental Association.

Adipose. Fat or fatty.

Alcohol. Ethanol. Ethyl alcohol. Distilled from the products of anaerobic fermentation of carbohydrate. An ingredient in a variety of beverages including beer, wine, liqueurs, cordials, and mixed or straight drinks. Pure alcohol itself yields about seven Calories per gram, of which more than 75 percent is available to the body.

Alkaline-forming foods. Foods in which the alkaline residue exceeds the acidic residue.

Alkalosis. An excess of base in the body, commonly resulting from persistent vomiting, excessive sodium bicarbonate intake, or hyperventilation. An abnormal condition of elevated blood pH caused by excessive loss of acids from the body without comparable loss of base or more supply of base than can be neutralized or eliminated.

Allergen. Any agent or substance (usually protein) capable of producing an allergic reaction.

Amino acid (AA). Chief components of proteins. Each amino acid molecule contains one or more amino group ($-NH_2$) and carboxyl group ($-COOH$). Amino acids may be acid, basic, or neutral.

Anabolism. Process of building simple substances into more complex substances.

Anemia. Deficiency in the circulating hemoglobin, red blood cells, or packed cell volume resulting in decreased capacity of the blood to carry oxygen. Macrocytic (large cell size) anemias may result from folacin and B_{12} deficiencies. Microcytic (small cell size), hypochromic (low color index) anemia may result from iron deficiency. Iron, protein, folic acid, vitamin B_{12}, and vitamin C are the major nutrients essential in blood formation.

Anorexia. Lack or loss of appetite for food.

Antibiotic. A substance that destroys or inhibits the growth of bacteria and other micro-organisms.

Antioxidant. A substance which delays or prevents oxidation.

Antivitamin. A substance which may inactivate or destroy a vitamin.

Anuria. Suppression or absence of urinary excretion.

Apatite. Complex calcium phosphate salt giving strength to bones.

Appetite. Natural desire or craving for food.

Arteriosclerosis. Hardening, thickening, and loss of elasticity of the inner walls of arteries and capillaries.

Artificial sweeteners. See saccharin, sorbitol, mannitol, and cyclamate.

Ascorbic acid. Reduced form of vitamin C; water soluble vitamin; prevents scurvy.

Ash. Mineral residue remaining after burning or oxidizing all organic matter.

As Purchased (AP). The weight of food before removing or trimming inedible parts.

Atherosclerosis. A fatty degeneration of the blood vessels and connective tissue of arterial walls. A kind of arteriosclerosis. The fatty deposits, including cholesterol, phospholipids, triglycerides, and other substances, decrease the internal channel size of the blood vessel.

Atony. Lack of normal tone or strength.

Atrophy. A wasting away of the cell, tissue, or organ.

Available. A nutrient that is in a form readily

absorbed by the digestive tract and usable by the body.

Avidin. A protein in raw egg white which binds with the B vitamin, biotin, and prevents its absorption from the digestive tract. Cooking inactivates avidin.

Avitaminosis. A condition due to inadequate vitamin intake or absorption, increased body require. ment, or antivitamins.

Azotemia uremia. Retention of urea or other nitrogenous substances in the urine.

Balance study. Quantitative method of measuring amount of a nutrient ingested and excreted to determine retention (positive balance) or loss (negative balance).

Basal metabolism. Energy expended at complete physical and mental rest (12-to-16 hours after food ingestion and in thermally neutral temperature). Includes energy for respiration, circulation, gastrointestinal contractions, muscle tone, body temperature, and organ function. Basal metabolic rate (BMR) for an adult is approximately one Calorie per kilogram body weight per hour.

Beikost. Foods other than milk or formula.

Beriberi. Nutritional deficiency of thiamin (vitamin B_1) resulting in loss of appetite, general weakness, progressive edema, polyneuritis, and enlarged heart.

Bile. A fluid produced in the liver, stored, and concentrated in the gallbladder, and emptied into the duodenum to aid in digestion of fat.

Biological value (BV). The efficiency of food protein in supplying amino acids in the proper amounts for protein synthesis in the body. For example, meat has a high biological value (HBV) and beans have a low value. The Thomas-Mitchell equation for calculating BV follows:

$$\%BV = 100\% \times \frac{N\ intake - [(FN - MN) + (UNEN)]}{N\ intake - (FN - MN)}$$

where N = nitrogen, FN = fecal nitrogen, MN = metabolic nitrogen, UN = urinary nitrogen, and EN = endogenous nitrogen.

Biotin. A member of the water-soluble vitamin B complex; aids in fixation of carbon dioxide in fatty acid synthesis. Widely distributed in foodstuffs and synthesized by intestinal bacteria. Deficiency may be induced by large amount of avidin, causing scaly dermatitis, muscle pains, general malaise, and depression.

Bland. Any food that is not irritating to the gastric mucosa.

Blood lipids. Primarily cholesterol, phospholipid, and triglyceride which are bound to protein and circulate in the plasma.

Blood sugar level (BSL). The level of glucose (blood sugar) per 100 ml blood.

Bowel. The intestines.

Bran. The outer layer of whole grain. It contains iron, phosphorus, B vitamins, and fiber. Fiber absorbs water, softens and increases the bulk of stools, and facilitates elimination.

Brat diet. Diet consisting of banana, rice, applesauce, and toast; prescribed for diarrhea, especially for infants and children.

Bulk. The indigestible portion of carbohydrates which cannot he hydrolyzed by gastrointestinal enzymes.

Bulking agent. A metabolically inert substance which increases food volume without increasing calories.

BUN. Blood urea nitrogen.

Caffeine. An alkaloidal purine in coffee, tea, and cola drinks. A cardiac and renal stimulant which produces varying pharmacologic responses.

Calciferol. Vitamin D_2. A fat soluble vitamin produced by ergosterol irradiation. Prevents rickets.

Calcium. A major mineral, essential in bone formation, blood clotting, muscle tone, and nerve function. Deficiency may result in rickets or possibly osteomalacia.

Caffeine. An alkaloidal purine in coffee, tea, and cola drinks. A cardiac and renal stimulant which produces varying pharmacologic responses.

Calciferol. Vitamin D2. A fat soluble vitamin produced by ergosterol irradiation. Prevents rickets.

Calcium. A major mineral, essential in bone formation, blood clotting, muscle tone, and nerve function. Deficiency may result in rickets or possibly osteomalacia.

Calorie. The amount of heat energy required to raise the temperature of one kilogram of water one degree Centigrade. This is the large Calorie, or kilocalorie as used in nutrition. Calories come from carbohydrate, protein, fat, alcohol, and alcohol derivatives (like sorbitol).

Calculus. Commonly called stone.

Carbohydrate. One of three major energy sources in food. Contains carbon, hydrogen, and oxygen. *Available carbohydrates*, such as sugar and starch, provide glucose and glycogen to the body and supply four Calories per gram. *Indigestible carbohydrate* is primarily indigestible plant cellulose.

Carob powder. A powder that looks and tastes like chocolate but does not contain lactose. It may be used as a substitute for chocolate on lactose and galactose restricted diets.

Carotene. Yellow-red plant pigment converted in the body to vitamin A. Two international units of betacarotene are equivalent to one international unit of vitamin A. Abundant in green leafy, and yellow vegetables.

Casein. A milk protein which can contain large amounts of lactose. A phosphoprotein.

Casein hydrolysate. Chemical decomposition of the principal protein of milk.

Catabolism. Opposite of anabolism. Metabolic process in which complex substances are broken down into simpler substances, usually yielding energy. Destructive metabolism.

Catecholamines. Chemicals synthesized in the brain, sympathetic nerve endings, peripheral tissues, and adrenal medulla.

Celiac disease. Malabsorptive syndrome due to sensitivity to gluten and resulting in decreased jejunal mucosa absorption of fat, carbohydrates, protein, vitamins, and minerals. See Wheat Elimination, paragraph 11-3.

Cellulose. The structural fibers in plants. Indigestible polysaccharide which provides bulk to the diet.

Cholecalciferol. Vitamin D_2. Initiates production of a calcium-binding protein.

Cholesterol. Fat-like steroid alcohol found in all tissues. It may be synthesized in the body, but is usually absorbed from the digestive tract in the presence of fat. It is excreted in bile. Foods of animal origin are dietary sources of cholesterol. It is a key part of the fatty deposits in the arterial wall in atherosclerosis.

Choline. A component of lecithin. Necessary for fat transport, preventing accumulation of fat in the liver. Occurs in all plant and animal cells and may be synthesized from glycine (an amino acid) in the presence of a methyl group.

Chylomicron. A blood lipoprotein containing primarily triglycerides from dietary fat and smaller amounts of cholesterol, phospholipid, and protein.

Chyluria. The presence of a fat globule emulsion, formed in the small intestine after digestion, in the urine giving it a milky appearance.

Clinical nutrition. That branch of the health sciences having to do with the diagnosis, treatment, and prevention of human disease caused by deficiency, excess, or metabolic imbalance of dietary nutrients.

Cobalamin. Vitamin B_{12}. Antipernicious anemia factor; extrinsic factor.

Coffee oils. Possible cause of gastrointestinal irritation, diarrhea is a common symptom.

Colloid. A material whose particles are between 1 and 100 millimicrons in size and dispersed throughout a medium. The particles in dispersion are larger than ordinary crystalloid molecules but are not large enough to settle out under the influence of gravity. Examples are blood protein and gelatin.

Connective tissue. Collagen and elastin. Collagen is converted to gelatin by moist heat cookery. Elastin is not broken down or softened in cooking.

Creatinine. One of the end products of food protein breakdown. The amount excreted in the urine is an index of muscle mass and may be used as a measure of basal heat production. **Clear liquid dessert.** Desserts that provide little or no residue, including plain gelatin and Popsicles.

Crystalloid. Small molecules dissolved in a medium such as salt dissolved in water. Other examples are Na^+, K^+, other electrolytes, BUN, uric acid, and creatinine dissolved in the blood.

Curds. The clumped part of curdled milk which contains lactose.

Cyanocobalamin. Vitamin B_{12}.

Cyclamates. A noncaloric sweetener with 30 to 60 times the sweet taste of sucrose. A sodium or calcium salt of cyclohexylsulfamic acid. Cyclamate was changed from the GRAS (generally recognized as safe by the Food and Drug Administration) list to drug status, permitting use only under medical supervision. A suspected carcinogen.

Dehydration. Removal of water from food, tissue, or substrate.

Dehydroascorbic acid. Oxidized vitamin C; biologically active; reversibly oxidized and reduced. **Deciliter.** One-tenth of a liter.

Denaturation. To change the chemical,

physical, or biologic properties of protein by heating, freezing, irradiation, pressure, or organic solvent application.

Dextrin. The intermediate product of starch breakdown; a polysaccharide.

Dialysis. To separate substances in a solution by using a semipermeable membrane; small substances will pass through and larger molecules will not. As used in food preparation, see attachment 5.

Diet. Food and drink consumed. See specific types in text.

Dietary consultation. Individualized professional guidance provided to assist patients in adapting food consumption to meet health needs. The patient's background, socioeconomic needs, and personal preferences are considered when instructing patients on the physician-prescribed diet.

Dietary history. Record of an individual's food intake taken by 24-hour recall or repeated food records. Basis for individualized dietary consultation.

Dietary status. Bodily condition resulting from the utilization of the essential nutrients available to the body. Dietary history provides some indication of dietary status.

Dietetics. The science and art of planning, preparing, and serving meals to individuals and groups according to the principles of nutrition and management; economic, social, cultural, psychological, and health or disease conditions are considered.

Dietitian. A professional who practices dietetics after following a prescribed academic program for a baccalaureate degree in an accredited institution and completing an accredited internship, or equivalent.

Dietitian, Registered (R.D.). A qualified dietitian who has also successfully completed the examination for professional registration and maintains continuing education requirements by completing 75 clock hours of professional education every 5 years.

Digestibility. The amount of nutrient absorbed by the body and not excreted in the feces.

Digestion. Process of converting food into substances which can be absorbed by the body.

Disaccharidase. An enzyme which hydrolyzes disaccharides to yield two single sugars.

Diuresis. Increased secretion of urine.

Dumping syndrome. Postgastrectomy epigastric discomfort resulting when a large amount of hypertonic, concentrated food draws large quantities of fluid from the bloodstream into the intestine.

Duodenum. The first segment of small intestine between the pylorus and jejunum. Pancreatic juice and bile are secreted into the duodenum.

Edible portion (EP). The trimmed weight of food that is normally eaten.

Effusion. Fluid escaping into a part or tissue.

Endogenous. Originating within the cell or tissue.

Endogenous protein. Body or tissue protein.

Energy. Capacity to do work, such as muscular activity, maintaining body temperature, and operating metabolic processes. As obtained from food oxidation, energy is expressed in calories.

Enrichment. The addition of one or more nutrients to a food to attain a higher level of those nutrients than normally present in the food. Bread and flour are often enriched.

Enteral. Within or by way of the intestine. Often used to refer to supplemental oral, or tube feedings.

Enzyme. An organic compound (usually protein) which accelerates metabolic reactions (such as digestion).

Epinephrine. A hormone released primarily in response to hypoglycemia. It increases blood pressure, stimulates the heart muscle, accelerates the heart rate, and increases cardiac output.

Ergosterol. A plant steroid converted to vitamin D_2, calciferol, upon irradiation or exposure to ultraviolet light.

Essential amino acid. Those amino acids that cannot be synthesized by the body; they must be obtained from food to ensure normal growth, development, and tissue repair.

Essential fatty acid. Fatty acids that cannot be synthesized in adequate amounts by the body to ensure growth, reproduction, skin health, and proper fat utilization.

Ethanol. See alcohol.

Ethylenediamine-tetraacetate. A non-nutritive food additive used to separate a part from a whole, or to act as a metal scavenger.

Exchange list. Grouping of foods similar in nutrients together so they may be used interchangeably.

Excipient. Any addition to a medicine designed to permit proper shaping or consistency.

Exogenous. Originating outside, externally caused. Extrinsic factor. Vitamin B_{12}.

Exudative enteropathics. Any disease of the intestine with material escaped from the blood vessels deposited in the intestine.

Fat. One of three major sources of food energy, which provides nine Calories per gram. A mixture of glyceryl esters of fatty acids; an oily, yellow, or white substance of animal or vegetable sources.

Fatty acid. Organic acids which combine with glycerol to form fat.

Favism. An acute hemolytic anemia resulting from ingestion of fava beans (horse or broad beans).

Ferment. Chemical change caused by digestive enzymes of micro-organisms.

Fiber. An indigestible part of fruits, vegetables, cereals, and grains important in the diet as roughage, or bulk.

Flatulence. Excessive gas in the stomach or intestines.

Focacin. Folic acid. Pteroylglutamic acid. A water-soluble vitamin of the B complex group needed for normal growth and hemopoiesis. Widely distributed in plant and animal tissues. Deficiency may be induced by sulfonamides or folic acid antagonists.

Food habit. Usual pattern of an individual or group for choosing, preparing, and eating food resulting from family, cultural, economic, and religious influences.

Fortification. The addition of one or more nutrients to a food whether or not they are naturally present. An example is margarine fortified with vitamin A.

Full liquid dessert. Desserts that are fluid or that easily become fluid, including plain gelatin, ice cream, soft custard, and pudding.

Galactose. A six carbon monosaccharide.

Galactosemia. Galactose in the blood due to an inborn error of metabolism in which the enzyme galactose-l-phosphate uridyl transferase is absent; thus, galactose is not converted to glucose. Mental and growth retardation, liver and spleen enlargement, cataracts, jaundice, weight loss, vomiting, and diarrhea result unless dietary modification eliminates lactose-and galactose-containing foods from the diet.

Gavage. Feeding via insertion of a tube through the mouth into the stomach.

Gelatin. An incomplete protein obtained from partial hydrolysis of collagen.

Geriatrics. Study and treatment of diseases and problems occurring in old age.

Glomerular filtration rate (GFR). Milliliters of blood which pass through the kidney glomeruli in one minute; may be used to estimate kidney function.

Glucose. Dextrose. Grape sugar. Blood sugar. A monosaccharide which may be absorbed into the bloodstream and is the major source of energy for the brain and nervous tissues.

Glutathione. A tripeptide believed to assist sulfhydryl containing enzymes to stay in the reduced state essential for their activity.

Gluten. A cereal grain protein; gluten provides elasticity to bread dough.

Glycogen. A polysaccharide composed of glucose units. The main form of carbohydrate stored by man and animals in liver, muscles, and other tissues.

Gram. A unit of mass and weight in the metric system. An ounce is approximately 28 grams.

Gravidity. Pregnancy.

Hemicellulose. A largely indigestible plant polysaccharide that absorbs water. Pectin is a hemi-cellulose that may lower serum cholesterol.

Hemodialysis. Dialyzing blood to remove waste products.

Hepatosplenomegaly. Enlargement of both liver and spleen.

High biological value (HBV) protein. A protein readily digested, absorbed, and utilized by the body, such as the protein in eggs.

Homeostasis. Balance of the internal environment including fluid, pH, body temperature, blood sugar level, heart and pulse rates, and hormonal control.

Hydrogenated oil. Addition of molecular hydrogen to double bonds in unsaturated fatty acids creating saturated solid fat with reduced essential fatty acid biological value.

Hypercholesterolemia. Elevated blood cholesterol associated with cardiovascular diseases.

Hyperchylomicronemia. Elevation of chylomicron lipoproteins circulating in the blood.

Hyperkalemia. Increased potassium in the blood. Hyperlipidemia. An elevation of one or

more lipid constituents of the blood.
Hyperlipoproteinemia. Elevation of blood lipoproteins.
Hypernatremia. Excessive amount of sodium in the blood.
Idiopathic. Without known origin.
Ileum. The part of the small intestine between the jejunum and large intestine.
Inborn error of metabolism. A metabolic defect existing at birth due to missing genes.
Incomplete protein. A protein lacking one or more essential amino acids.
Ingestion. Eating or drinking; taking in.
Inorganic. Minerals that do not contain carbon.
Inositol. A water soluble alcohol found primarily in cereal grains which combines with phosphate to form phytic acid.
Instant cereal. Pregelatinized (precooked) cereal requiring addition of water before serving.
Insulin. A hormone secreted by the beta cells of the islets of Langerhans in the pancreas. It is essential to carbohydrate metabolism in the body. Exogenous insulin is injected by some diabetics to provide proper carbohydrate metabolism.
Insulin shock (or) reaction. Very low blood sugar level resulting from overdose of insulin. Symptoms include hunger, weakness, nervousness, double vision, shallow breathing, sweating, headache, dizziness, mental confusion, muscular twitching, convulsion, loss of consciousness, coma, and eventually death. Fruit juice or intravenous glucose are often used to counteract insulin reaction.
International unit. A measure of biologic activity of a nutrient.
Interpolate. To determine intermediate values in a series based on observed values or to introduce new material in a given subject.
Intrinsic factor. Chemical in gastric juice that facilitates vitamin B_{12} (extrinsic factor) absorption. Lack of intrinsic factor results in pernicious anemia.
Iodine. A trace mineral essential in regulating basal metabolism. Deficiency results in goiter.
Iodine number (or) value. The number of grams of iodine absorbed by 100 grams of fat. Indicates the amount of fatty acids and degree of unsaturation of a fat. The iodine number of saturated coconut oil is 10, and that of polyunsaturated safflower oil is 100.

Iodized salt. Table salt with one part sodium or potassium iodide per 5,000 to 10,000 parts sodium chloride.
Irradiation. Exposure to ultraviolet rays used for destroying microorganisms in food and converting provitamin D to active vitamin D.
Isocaloric. Containing an equal number of Calories.
Jejunum. The part of the small intestine between the duodenum and ileum.
Joule. A metric measure of energy equaling 4.184 Calories.
Junket. The precipitated protein of milk casein and fat.
Ketogenic-antiketogenic ratio. The ratio of the amount of ketogenic factors, such as fatty acids and ketogenic amino acids, to the amount of anti-ketogenic factors, such as carbohydrates, glucogenic amino acids, and the glycerol of fat.
Ketosis. An accumulation of ketone bodies (beta-hydroxybutyric acid, acetoacetic acid, and acetone) from incomplete fatty acid oxidation. Uncontrolled ketosis may result in acidosis.
Kosher foods. Foods prepared and served by Orthodox Judaism dietary laws which include: (1) milk and meat are not consumed at the same meal, (2) meat must be slaughtered in a special ordained manner and cleaned (koshered) by soaking in water, salting, and washing, (3) meat from cud-chewing, cloven-hooved animals (cows, sheep, goats) may be eaten, (4) finfish may be eaten. No pork or shellfish are eaten.
Kwashiorkor. Severe protein malnutrition in children resulting in retarded growth, anemia, edema, fatty liver, lack of pigment in the hair and skin, gastrointestinal disorders, muscle atrophy, and psychomotor wasting.
Labile. Unstable.
Lactase. Enzyme that splits lactose to glucose and galactose.
Lactate, lactic acid, lactalbumin. Substances related to lactose but which cannot be changed into galactose by the body.
Lacto-ovo-vegetarian. Person subsisting on grains, legumes, vegetables, fruits, milk, and eggs. Meat, poultry and fish are avoided.
Lactose. "Milk sugar." Disaccharide occurring in milk products. Contains one glucose and one galactose group.
Lactose intolerance. Lactose malabsorption due to lactase deficiency. Results in

Lecithin. Phosphatidyl choline. A phospholipid containing glycerol, fatty acids, phosphoric acid, and choline. Involved in fat transport, lecithin is found in many cells, especially nerves. Lecithin synthesis in the body depends upon dietary intake of methyl groups or choline.

Leucine. An essential amino acid with ketogenic properties.

Licorice. Black flavoring extract containing glycyrrhizic acid which, in large amounts, can cause hypertension and hypokalemia.

Lignin. A constituent of crude fiber. An indigestible cellulose. With cellulose, the principal Part of the woody plants. Unlike cellulose, lignin can combine with bile to form insoluble complexes which are not absorbed.

Linoleic acid. Polyunsaturated essential fatty acid with 18 carbon atoms and two double bonds.

Linolenic acid. A nonessential polyunsaturated fatty acid with 18 carbon atoms and three double bonds.

Lipid. Fat or fat-like substances. Includes fatty acids, triglycerides, phosphatides (such as lecithin), terpenes, and steroids (such as cholesterol).

Lipoprotein. A compound consisting of a simple protein and lipid and involved in lipid transport. Types of lipoprotein circulating in the blood include chylomicrons, alpha lipoproteins (high density lipoproteins, HDL), prebeta lipoproteins (very low density lipoproteins, VLDL), and beta lipoprotein (low density lipoprotein, LDL). All are composed of phospholipid, triglyceride, cholesterol, and protein.

Long-chain fatty acid. Fatty acids containing 12 or more carbon atoms, such as stearic (18 carbon) and palmatic (16 carbon) acids.

Low sodium milk. Milk processed by ion-exchange process to remove approximately 90 percent of the naturally occurring sodium. Thiamin, riboflavin, and calcium are also decreased with an increase in potassium.

Lycine. An essential amino acid and the limiting amino acid in many cereal products.

Magnesium. An essential mineral. A cofactor in metabolism.

Malabsorption syndrome. A condition caused by failure of the body to absorb nutrients such as fats, calcium and other minerals, and vitamins. Examples include celiac disease, chronic pancrea-titis, sprue, cystic fibrosis, and carbohydrate intolerance.

Malnutrition. Lack or excess of absorbed nutrients resulting in impaired health status.

Manganese. An essential trace mineral.

Mannitol. A partially absorbed sugar alcohol with a sweet taste equal to sugar but with half the calories.

Maple syrup urine disease. Inborn error of metabolism treated with dietary restriction of leucine. isoleucine, and valine.

Marasmus. Severe protein-calorie malnutrition of infants and young children.

Medium chain fatty acid. Fatty acids containing 8 to 10 carbon atoms, such as caprylic (8 carbon) and capric (10 carbon) acids.

Medium chain triglyceride (MCT). A fat composed primarily of saturated fatty acids with 8 to 10 carbon atoms. A commercially prepared food product for persons not able to digest or absorb food fats and oils.

Menadione. A synthetic, vitamin K_2 is much more potent biologically than vitamin K.

Metabolism. Chemical changes in the body: anabolism and catabolism.

Methionine. An essential amino acid important in protein and fat, metabolism.

Methylcellulose. Indigestible polysaccharide which provides bulk and satiety without. calories.

Micronutrient. Nutrients present. in less than 0.005 percent of body weight, such as trace minerals. Also, nutrients present in very small amounts in food.

Microgram. A metric system unit of mass representing one one-millionth of a gram or one one-thousandth of a milligram.

Milk-alkali syndrome. Ingestion of large quantities of milk and alkalies resulting in hypercalcemia, calcium in soft tissues, vomiting, gastrointestinal bleeding, and high blood pressure.

Milliosmole. One thousandth of an osmole.

Mineral. Inorganic elements that build and repair body tissue or control body functions. The ones known to be essential to man are calcium, chlorine, chromium, cobalt, copper, fluorine, iodine, iron, magnesium, manganese, molybdenum, phosphorus, potassium, selenium, sodium, sulfur. and zinc.

Mineral oil. Liquid petroleum substance which is not absorbed by the gastrointestinal tract but interferes with absorption of fat soluble vitamins.

Monosaccharides. Carbohydrates composed of single simple sugars that cannot be hydrolyzed (broken) into smaller units. Examples are fructose, galactose, glucose, and ribose.

Monounsaturated fat. Fat that neither raises nor lowers blood cholesterol. Examples are olive oil and peanut oil.

Monounsaturated fatty acid. Fatty acids with only one unsaturated double bond.

Monosodium glutamate (MSG). A sodium-containing flavoring used in Asian cookery.

Nasogastric tube. Used in tube feeding; a tube inserted via the nose and esophagus into the stomach.

Nausea. Stomach discomfort with a tendency to vomit.

Negative nitrogen balance. Daily nitrogen excretion greater than nitrogen intake which may be brought about by fever, surgery, or burns.

Niacin. Nicotenic acid. A water-soluble B complex vitamin. Antipellagra factor. Necessary to cell respiration, carbohydrate and protein metabolism, and lipid synthesis; thus, requirement varies with caloric intake.

Niacin equivalent. The sum of nicotinic acid and niacin is the niacin equivalent. Sixty milligrams tryptophan may be converted to one milligram nicotinic acid.

Nicotinic acid. Niacin.

Nitrogen balance/equilibrium. An individual is in nitrogen balance when the nitrogen intake from food protein each day is approximately equal to the nitrogen loss in feces and urine.

Non-nutritive sweetener. A noncaloric synthetic sugar substitute. Examples are saccharine and cyclamate.

Norepinephrine. A hormone released primarily in response to hypotension to raise blood pressure.

Nutrient. Any chemical substance useful in nutrition for providing heat and energy, building and repairing tissues, and regulating life processes.

Nutrition. The study of food in relation to health. Combination of processes by which the body receives and uses the materials necessary for body functions, energy, growth, and tissue renewal.

Nutrition history. Laboratory and clinical findings, and a dietary history.

Nutritional status. The condition of the body resulting from consumption and utilization of nutrients.

Nutriture. Tissue nutrient balance of supply and demand.

Obesity. Fat. Body weight approximately 20 percent or more above desirable weight due to adiposity.

Oil. A lipid that is liquid at room temperature.

Oleic acid. An 18 carbon monounsaturated fatty acid abundant in fats and oils.

Oliguria. Decreased urinary output in relation to fluid intake.

Oral hypoglycemic agents. Orally administered compounds that stimulate beta cells in the islands of Langerhans of the pancreas to secrete endogenous insulin that reduces blood glucose in diabetics. Contraindicated for some patients.

Osmolality. A property of a solution which depends on the concentration of the solute per unit of solvent.

Osmolarity. A property of a solution which depends on the concentration of the solute per unit of total volume of solution.

Osmole. The standard unit of osmotic pressure. Overweight. Fat. Body weight approximately 10 to 20 percent above desirable weight due to adiposity.

Oxalate. Salt of oxalic acid. When combined in insoluble calcium salts. oxalate renders calcium unavailable for absorption.

Pancreatic juice. A digestive juice produced by the pancreas and secreted into the duodenum; contains enzymes involved in digestion of protein, carbohydrate. and fat.

Pantothenic acid. A water-soluble B complex vitamin that is part of coenzyme A. It is essential for growth. normal skin. nervous system development, and adrenal cortex function.

Papain. A proteolytic enzyme of papaya often used as a meat tenderizer.

Parenteral feeding. Food provided without use of the mouth and digestive tract, such as intravenous feeding.

Pasteurized. Heat treated to kill most pathogenic microorganisms. For example. pasteurized eggnog prevents the potential of salmonella infection from eggnog made with raw eggs.

Pellagra. Multiple B vitamin deficiency, notably

of niacin. Symptoms include dermatitis, diarrhea, dementia, and death.

Peristalsis. Alternate contraction and relaxation pf the gastrointestinal tract which moves contents toward the anus.

Pernicious anemia. Chronic macrocytic anemia due to B_{12} and intrinsic factor deficiency.

pH. A measure of acidity and alkalinity.

Phenylalanine. An essential amino that may be converted to tyrosine. It can be ketogenic, glycogenic, and participate in transamination.

Phenylketonuria (PKU). Inborn error in metabolism resulting in the lack of the enzyme phenylal-anine hydroxylase. Phenylalanine cannot be converted to tyrosine without this enzyme. The resultant high levels of phenylalanine result in permanent mental retardation and poor growth and development unless there is close dietary control of phenylalanine ingestion.

Phosphorus. An essential mineral.

Polysaccharide. A complex carbohydrate containing more than four monosaccharides. Examples are glycogen, starch, and cellulose.

Polyunsaturated fatty acids (PUFA). Fatty acids with more than one unsaturated bond in the molecule.

Polyunsaturated: saturated fatty acid ratio (P/S ratio). The relative amount of polyunsaturated linoleic acid to total saturated fatty acids.

Positive nitrogen balance. Nitrogen intake exceeds nitrogen output, such as during infancy and childhood (tissue anabolism).

Potassium. An essential mineral of the intracellular fluids.

Pressor agent. Any substance that raises blood pressure.

Protein. The primary structure of plant and animal bodies. It is composed of amino acids and is approximately 16 percent nitrogen. Protein provides four Calories per gram.

Protein hydrolysate. A mixture of "predigested protein" in the form of amino acids and polypep-tides. Used for oral or parenteral feeding in cases of impaired digestion, such as pancreatic diseases.

Protein calorie malnutrition. A condition of severe tissue wasting, subcutaneous fat loss, and dehydration caused by inadequate protein and calorie intake.

Protein quality. A complete protein contains all the essential amino acids for growth and life. A partial protein maintains life but not growth. An incomplete protein can support neither growth nor life. If two incomplete proteins each supply the limiting amino acid(s) of the other, together they may be capable of supporting growth and life.

Protein-sparing. Refers to calories supplied by carbohydrates and fat. These calories save protein from being "burned" as energy so it may be used for anabolism.

Provitamin. A substance related to a vitamin but with no vitamin activity until it is converted to the biologically active form.

P/S ratio. Ratio of polyunsaturated to saturated fatty acids.

Pureed. A food blenderized to a paste consistency. Most baby foods are pureed.

Purine. Nitrogenous compounds of dietary or endogenous origin catabolized to uric acid in the body.

Pyridoxine. An alcohol form of vitamin 136, a B complex vitamin.

Quick-cooking cereal/rice. Cereals and rice that have disodium phosphate added to reduce their preparation time.

Raffinose. Trisaccharide containing glucose, galactose, and fructose. It is found in beets, roots, underground stems, cottonseed meal, and molasses.

Recommended (Daily) Dietary Allowances (RDA). Suggested amounts of nutrients to provide when planning diets. Designed to maintain good nutrition in healthy persons of average build and activity in a temperature climate with a margin of safety 10 to 50 percent above normal dietary requirements.

Reconstitute. To restore to the normal state, usually by adding water.

Refuse. Inedible, discarded foodstuffs.

Residue. Amount of bulk remaining in the digestive tract after digestion and absorption.

Retinol. A vitamin A alcohol.

Retinol equivalent (RE). Unit expressing vitamin A activity. One RE = 1 u retinol, 6 u beta-carotene, and 12 u for other provitamin A carotenoids.

Riboflavin. Vitamin B_2. Heat stable, water soluble vitamin essential to the health of skin and eyes.

Rickets. Vitamin D deficiency or disturbance of calcium-phosphorus metabolism.

Saccharin. A noncaloric artificial sweetener 700 times sweeter than sugar.

Salt. Table salt; sodium chloride; NaCl.

Satiety. Sense of fullness or comfort; gratification of appetite.

Saturated fat. A fat with no double bonds; chemically satisfied. Often solid at room temperature and usually of animal origin. Examples are butter, lard, and steak fat.

Scurvy. Vitamin C deficiency disease resulting in swollen bleeding gums, hemorrhage of the skin and mucous membranes, and anemia.

Secretagogue. An agent that stimulates secretion.

Short-chain fatty acid. Those containing four to six carbon atoms, such as caproic (6 carbon) and butyric (4 carbon) acids. Yields only about 5 Calories per gram.

Skinfold measurement. Measurement of the thickness of skin at body sites where adipose is normally deposited. Measured with a caliper and compared against a standard chart, it provides an estimate of degree of fatness.

Sodium. An essential mineral important in extra-cellular body fluids and in regulating many body functions.

Soft. Any easily digested food that is soft in texture and provides no harsh fibers or connective tissue.

Sorbitol. A sugar alcohol apparently metabolized without insulin. It contains 4 calories per gram and can be converted to utilizable carbohydrate in the form of glucose. Excessive use may cause gastrointestinal discomfort and diarrhea.

Specific dynamic action. Increased metabolism from heat of digesting, absorbing, and metabolizing food. Approximately 30 percent for protein, 13 percent, for fat, and 4 to 5 percent for carbohydrate.

Standard of identity of foods. Standards established by a government agency, primarily the US Food and Drug Administration, to define quality and container fill for foods.

Stachyose. Tetrasaccharide containing glucose, fructose, and two molecules of galactose. It is found in tubers, peas, lima beans, and beets.

Starch. Plant storage form of carbohydrate (just as the animal storage form is glycogen). A complex polysaccharide. Food sources include breads, cereals, and starchy vegetables.

Sucrose. Table sugar. A disaccharide composed of glucose and fructose.

Sugar. Sucrose. A sweet, soluble carbohydrate that provides 4 Calories of energy per gram.

Sulphur. An essential mineral.

Supplement. A concentrated source of nutrients, such as vitamins or minerals.

Supplementary feeding. Food provided in addition to regular meals to increase nutrient intake.

Sweetening agent (or) sweeteners. Natural sweeteners, such as sugar, or synthetic sweeteners, such as saccharin.

Synthesis. Putting elements together to form a whole.

Tea tannin. Possible cause of constipation.

Textured vegetable protein. Vegetable protein that is flavored, colored, and textured to resemble meat and poultry products.

Theobromine. The alkaloidal stimulant in cocoa beans, tea leaves, and cola nuts that acts as a diuretic, arterial dilator, and myocardial stimulant.

Thiamin. Vitamin B_2, a B complex vitamin and part of a coenzyme important in carbohydrate metabolism. Prevents beriberi.

Threonine. An essential amino acid.

Tocopherols. An alcohol-like group of substances. Four forms have vitamin E activity.

Tofu. Soybean curd; usually available in oriental grocery stores.

Trace minerals. Minerals required by the body in minute amounts.

Triglyceride. A fat composed of a glycerol molecule with three fatty acids.

Tryptophane. An essential amino acid. May be converted to niacin, and a source of the vasoconstrictor serotonin.

Tyramine. A decarboxylation product of tyrosine found in fermented cheeses, wines, and other foods. Produces severe hypertensive reaction if consumed in conjunction with monoamine oxidase inhibitory drugs.

Underweight. Body weight 10 percent or more below the established standards.

Unsaturated fatty acids. Those with one or more double bonds. Abundant in vegetable oils.

Urea. Major nitrogen containing product of protein metabolism and chief nitrogenous constituent of the urine.

Uremia. A toxic condition caused by the retention in the blood of urinary constituents including urea, creatine, uric acid, and other end products of protein metabolism.

Vasopressor. Any agent that causes contraction of the muscular tissue lining the arteries and capillaries.

Vegetarian (or) vegan. Person subsisting entirely or in a large part on fruits, grains, legumes, and vegetables. If eggs, fish, meat, milk, and poultry are totally excluded, a vegetarian diet may be deficient in calcium, phosphorus, riboflavin, and vitamins B_{12} and D. Pure vegetarian diets are usually inadequate in protein for children.

Viosterol. Vitamin D_2, a product of ergosterol irradiation.

Vitamin. Organic substance provided in minute amounts in food or endogenuously synthesized. Essential in metabolic functions.

Vitamin A. Fat-soluble vitamin necessary for normal skin and bone development, maintenance of vision, and synthesis of mucopolysaccharides.

Vitamin B complex. Water soluble vitamins often found together in nature. Vitamins B_1 (thiamin), B_2 (riboflavin), B_6 group (pyridoxine, pyridoxal, and pyridoxamine), B_{12} group (cobalamins), nicotinic acid (niacin), pteroylglutamic acid (PGA, folacin, or folic acid), pantothenic acid, and biotin. All except B_{12} are coenzymes.

Vitamin C. Water-soluble vitamin. Ascorbic acid.

Vitamin D. Fat-soluble vitamins including ergocalciferol (D_2) and cholecalciferol (D_3).

Vitamin E. Fat-soluble vitamin. Tocopherols.

Vitamin K. Fat-soluble vitamin consumed in food and produced endogenously by intestinal flora. Necessary for blood clotting.

Water. A major nutrient required by the body. Endogenous water is provided as a byproduct of metabolism. Exogenous water may be in the fluid form or contained in food.

Water requirement. Water functions by removing body heat and urinary excreta. One milliliter water per calorie is usually sufficient unless there is a pathological condition such as fever or burn.

Whey. A clear, watery liquid remaining when milk curdles. It contains lactose, but little or no fat.

Zanthine. Weakly basic alkaloid chemicals including caffeine, theophylline, and theobromine.

Zinc. An essential trace mineral involved in growth, digestion, and metabolism. Deficiency results in retarded growth, delayed sexual maturity, and delayed wound healing.